Imagine Life God's Way

Parables

New Community Bible Study Series

Exodus: Journey Toward God
Acts: Build Community
Romans: Find Freedom
Philippians: Run the Race
Colossians: Discover the New You
James: Live Wisely
1 Peter: Stand Strong
1 John: Love Each Other
Parables: Imagine Life God's Way
Sermon on the Mount 1: Connect with God
Sermon on the Mount 2: Connect with Others
Revelation: Experience God's Power

JOHN ORTBERG
WITH KEVIN & SHERRY HARNEY

New Community
KNOWING. LOVING. SERVING. CELEBRATING.

Imagine Life God's Way

PARABLES

GRAND RAPIDS, MICHIGAN 49530

We want to hear from you. Please send your comments about this book to us in care of the address below. Thank you.

GRAND RAPIDS, MICHIGAN 49530

www.zondervan.com

ZONDERVAN™

Parables: Imagine Life God's Way

Requests for information should be addressed to:

Zondervan, *Grand Rapids, Michigan 49530*

ISBN: 0-310-22881-6

Interior design by Sherri Hoffman

Printed in the United States of America

05 06 07 /❖ CH/ 10 9 8 7

CONTENTS

God has created us for community. This need is built into the very fiber of our being, the DNA of our spirit. As Christians, our deepest desire is to see the truth of God's Word as it influences our relationships with others. We long for a dynamic encounter with God's Word, intimate closeness with His people, and radical transformation of our lives. But how can we accomplish those three difficult tasks?

The New Community Bible Study Series creates a place for all of this to happen. In-depth Bible study, community-building opportunities, and life-changing applications are all built into every session of this small group study guide.

How to Build Community

How do we build a strong, healthy Christian community? The whole concept for this study grows out of a fundamental understanding of Christian community that is dynamic and transformational. We believe that Christians don't simply gather to exchange doctrinal affirmations. Rather, believers are called by God to get into each other's lives. We are family, for better or for worse, and we need to connect with each other.

Community is not built through sitting in the same building and singing the same songs. It is forged in the fires of life. When we know each other deeply—the good, the bad, and the ugly—community is experienced. Community grows when we learn to rejoice with one another, celebrating life. Roots grow deep when we know we are loved by others and are free to extend love to them as well. Finally, community deepens and is built when we commit to serve each other and let others serve us. This process of doing ministry and humbly receiving the ministry of others is critical for healthy community life.

Build Community Through Knowing and Being Known

We all long to know others deeply and to be fully known by them. Although we might run from this level of intimacy at times, we all want to have people in our lives who trust us enough to disclose the deep and tender parts of themselves. In turn, we want to reveal some of our feelings, expressing them freely to people we trust.

The first section of each of these six studies creates a place for deep knowing and being known. Through serious reflection on the truth of Scripture, you will be invited to communicate parts of your heart and life with your small group members. You might even discover yourself opening parts of your heart that you have thus far kept hidden. The Bible study and discussion questions do not encourage surface conversation. The only way to go deep in knowing others and being known by them is to dig deep, and this takes some work. Knowing others also takes trust—that you will honor each other and respect each other's confidences.

Build Community Through Celebrating and Being Celebrated

If you have not had a good blush recently, read a short book in the Bible called Song of Songs. It's a record of a bride and groom writing poetic and romantic love letters to each other. They are freely celebrating every conceivable aspect of each other's personality, character, and physical appearance. At one point the groom says, "You have made my heart beat fast with a single glance from your eyes." Song of Songs is a reckless celebration of life, love, and all that is good.

We need to recapture the joy and freedom of celebration. In every session of this study, your group will commit to celebrate together. Although there are many ways to express joy, we will let our expression of celebration come through prayer. In each session you will take time to come before the God of joy and celebrate who He is and what He is doing. You will also have opportunity to celebrate what God is doing in your life and the lives of those who are a part of your small group. You will become a community of affirmation, celebration, and joy through your prayer time together.

You will need to be sensitive during this time of prayer together. Not everyone feels comfortable praying with a group of people. Be aware that each person is starting at a different place in their freedom to pray in a group, and be patient. Seek to promote a warm and welcoming atmosphere where each person can stretch a little and learn what it means to be a community that celebrates with God in the center.

Build Community Through Loving and Being Loved

Unless we are exchanging deeply committed levels of love with a few people, we will die slowly on the inside. This is precisely why so many people feel almost nothing at all. If we don't learn to exchange love with family and friends, we will eventually grow numb and no longer believe love is even a possibility. This is not God's plan. He hungers for us to be loved and to give love to others. As a matter of fact, He wants this for us even more than we want it for ourselves.

Every session in this study will address the area of loving and being loved. You will be challenged, in your personal life and as a small group, to be intentional and consistent about building love relationships. You will get practical tools and be encouraged to set measurable goals for giving and receiving love.

Build Community Through Serving and Being Served

Community is about serving and humbly allowing others to serve you. The single most stirring example of this is recorded in John 13, where Jesus takes the position of the lowest servant and washes the feet of His followers. He gives them a powerful example and then calls them to follow. Servanthood is at the very core of community. To sustain deep relationships over a long period of time, there must be humility and a willingness to serve each other.

At the close of each session will be a clear challenge to servanthood. As a group, and as individual followers of Christ, you will discover that community is built through serving others. You will also find that your own small group members will grow in their ability to extend service to your life.

Bible Study Basics

To get the most out of this study, you will need to prepare and participate. Here are some guidelines to help you.

Preparing for the Study

1. If possible, even if you are not the leader, look over each session before you meet, read the Bible passages, and answer the questions. The more you are prepared, the more you will gain from the study.
2. Begin your preparation time with prayer. Ask God to help you understand the passage and apply it to your life.
3. A good modern translation, such as the *New International Version,* the *New American Standard Bible,* or the *New Revised Standard Version,* will give you the most help. Questions in this guide are based on the *New International Version.*
4. Read and reread the passages. You must know what the passage says before you can understand what it means and how it applies to you.
5. Write your answers in the spaces provided in the study guide. This will help you participate more fully in the discussion and will also help you personalize what you are learning.
6. Keep a Bible dictionary handy to look up unfamiliar words, names, or places.

Participating in the Study

1. Be willing to join in the discussion. The leader of the group will not be lecturing but will encourage people to discuss what he or she has learned in the passage. Plan to share what God has taught you during your preparation time.
2. Stick to the passages being studied. Base your answers on the verses being discussed rather than on outside authorities such as commentaries or your favorite author or speaker.

3. Try to be sensitive to the other members of the group. Listen attentively when they speak, and be affirming whenever you can. This will encourage more hesitant members of the group to participate.
4. Be careful not to dominate the discussion. By all means participate, but allow others to have equal time.
5. If you are a discussion leader or a participant who wants further insights, you will find additional comments in the Leader's Notes at the back of this book.

INTRODUCTION

Parables: Imagine Life God's Way

One of the problems about being around smart people is that they often let you know just how smart they are. There is an old story about Albert Einstein that may be true or simply legend, but it is a wonderful story. It is about him and his chauffeur. After traveling for months and the chauffeur hearing the same lecture over and over and over again, he said to Einstein, "I have heard you give that lecture so many times I could give it for you." Einstein responded, "Then why don't you!" And they decided to switch places for one evening.

The chauffeur did quite well and gave the whole lecture. Everything seemed to be going pretty well until it came time for the question-and-answer section of the evening. Someone stood up and asked a very complex question about quantum physics. The chauffeur stood for a minute and said nothing.

Finally he looked at the crowd and said, "That question is so easy I'm going to let my chauffeur answer it!"

Smart people can often work hard to let you know how smart they are. By contrast, Jesus is quite different. In Jesus we meet the wisest man who ever lived, but He did not have to prove Himself to anyone.

Jesus never showed off! He never made a point of trying to impress people with His brilliance. His desire was simply to help everyone to learn and to live in the truth. He hungered for men, women, and children to enter into the truth of God that He came to reveal.

Jesus was the smartest and wisest man who ever lived. He talked about God, the human heart, the future, life, anger, love, and everything that mattered. Those who heard Him were struck by the fact that Jesus had deep understanding about everything of consequence in life.

When the Bible talks about putting faith in Jesus, a big part of this is understanding that He is right! Jesus is right about everything—not just about how human beings get to heaven, but about every topic of life He addressed.

There is no question that Jesus gave considerable thought to His method of teaching. How would He engage great minds and feed the simple and uneducated people all at the same time? The primary method He chose for teaching was telling stories. In fact, about a third of his words recorded in the Bible are parables. In Matthew 13:34 we read, "Jesus spoke all these things to the crowd in parables; he did not say anything to them without using a parable." The parables are designed to help get the truth to everyone.

The actual linguistic background of the word parable comes from a compound word in Greek. One word is *ballo* (which means "to throw") and the other is *para* (which is a preposition that means "alongside of"). The sense is "to throw alongside of." The idea of a parable is that Jesus took an everyday occurrence, something that everyone was familiar with, and then He would throw it alongside a concept about the kingdom of God. By doing this, His hope was that everyone could learn the truth about God and His kingdom.

Jesus would say things like, "Have you ever seen a poor woman desperately searching for a lost coin? Have you ever seen a shepherd searching for a lost sheep? Then you understand about my heart for lost people." Jesus would tell stories about corrupt judges and plucky widows, about buried treasures and lazy employees and bad debts and noisy neighbors, and people got it! They flocked to Him. They longed to understand the truth of God that their hearts hungered to receive.

Jesus taught what I call "Christianity Illustrated." If a picture is worth a thousand words, Jesus spoke volumes through His stories. Jesus told colorful, unforgettable, compelling, culturally relevant stories. For two thousand years these stories have stretched the greatest minds in the world and they have fed the simplest ones. They have pierced the hardest hearts and shaped the greatest souls that have walked the face of the earth.

The Hebrew word for parable is *mashal*. It means "a riddle" or "a puzzle." A parable was something you had to think about. Sometimes the hearer would listen to the story, yet its full message would not set in. Later that day or week, the hearer might all of a sudden say "Aha!" and would realize that the story had been about them and they had not even known it! These stories were Jesus' way to get past people's natural defenses and reach their hearts.

The parables are at the core of what Jesus taught. This six-session study will help you begin to dig deeply into this storehouse of God's wisdom and truth.

If you are open and ready for what God wants to do in your heart through this study of the parables, Jesus will do what only He can do—He will be your teacher, He will stretch your mind, He will pierce your heart, He will shape your soul. And if you let the Spirit speak, you will begin to know God in new and fresh ways.

SESSION ONE

Overcoming Growth Barriers

MATTHEW 13:3–23

I remember when we brought Laura, our first child, home from the hospital. I was struck by the rapid rate of her growth. At the hospital she weighed only about six pounds. She was a tiny thing! But she ate and ate and ate in unbelievable quantities. Over the first year of her life she gained twelve pounds and basically tripled her weight. Even when I found out that this growth rate is pretty common for babies, I was still amazed!

I was so impressed by this rapid growth, in fact, that I sat down and figured out what would happen if she continued on this growth curve every year. Believe it or not, our little baby girl would have weighed 486 pounds by the time she turned four!

I remember visiting friends of ours who had a nine-month-old baby. They were waiting with excitement and anticipation for the little guy to learn how to walk. Now, when you think about it, walking is a pretty common thing. Billions of people do it every day. Yet when it happened to their child, this mom and dad were cheering like it was the first time in the history of the world that anyone had walked. To them it was a miracle. They smiled, laughed, and coaxed him along. This was big stuff!

Making the Connection

1. Describe a time when you saw positive growth or development in some area of your life.

Read Matthew 13:3–9

2. In this parable, the sower and the seed are constant; they don't change. The variable in this story is the soil. Describe the four kinds of soil in this parable and what happened to the seed that fell on each kind of soil.

Failure to Thrive

There is actually a medical designation for babies who are not growing and developing as they should be. Doctors will write on a chart "FTT," which means "failure to thrive." Thriving is the natural condition of human beings. It is what a life is created by God to do. When there is a failure to thrive, doctors seek to identify the barrier to growth and remove it so that life will begin to thrive once more.

This is also very true in the spiritual realm. God has made us to grow, to thrive, to flourish spiritually. God wants us to love someone tomorrow that we could not love yesterday. God wants sin to have less and less control of us as the years pass by. God longs that we would share our faith more and more freely and with greater boldness and effectiveness simply because it is so central to our lives. He wants us to pray more deeply, speak more truthfully, rejoice more fully, and forgive more freely with every passing year. When we come to the end of our life, God wants people to say, "That person walked with God."

Read Matthew 13:18–23

3. What are some of the barriers Jesus identifies in this parable that can cause a person to "fail to thrive"?

The Problem of Hard-Heartedness

Jesus said some seed fell along the path. In Jesus' day there were often hard-packed paths that ran near fields. Farmers and animals would walk on these paths. If seed fell on this kind of a hard surface, there was no chance it would grow. Jesus was saying that growth requires soil that is soft. If we replace the word soil with heart, we begin to understand the message Jesus was trying to convey.

Jesus understands that there are many people who have become hard-hearted toward God. These people have been disappointed, stepped on, and hurt a lot in life. They have become cynical and bitter and have allowed a protective coat to form around their heart so that God's seeds cannot penetrate. At this time, the evil one comes and snatches the seed away.

Knowing the meaning behind this parable should move us to do a "soil analysis" of our own heart. We need to be honest about whether our heart is hard, and do all we can to grow soft toward God.

Read Matthew 13:10–17

4. Jesus draws from the teaching of Isaiah as He portrays the condition of the human heart. How do you feel when you hear what Jesus says about the heart condition of human beings?

5. What is one life experience or lesson that has helped to soften your heart toward the things of God?

The Problem of Shallow Soil

In Jesus' day much of the soil was rocky and shallow. Much of the area that was used as farmland had only a few inches of topsoil over a rocky base. In many places, when roots would begin to spread and look for nutrition, all they would find was rock. Jesus wants us to know that growth requires soil that is soft and deep.

As we begin to do a soil analysis in our lives we may want to ask, "Is my faith putting down deep roots?" In his book *A Celebration of Discipline,* Richard Foster writes, "Superficiality is the curse of this age." We live in a world of shallow relationships, superficial conversations, hurried moments of prayer, too much television, and light commitments.

This kind of shallowness has also invaded the church. We have all met people who go to church and have every appearance of a real love and devotion for God, but have no depth. Bouncing from one spiritual activity to another with great enthusiasm may make it seem like we are grabbing onto everything in the spiritual life with great gusto; however, at the end of the day, there are no deep roots.

6. Most cars have warning lights that come on to let us know when something is about to break down or overheat. What are some of the warning lights that go off in your heart when the roots of your faith are not going down deep into the things of God?

If you did a root analysis on your own life right now, where would you put yourself on the graph below?

0	5	10
My roots have no depth.	My roots are in the soil of God's presence, but need to be much deeper.	My roots are deep in the things of God.

7. What is one exercise, activity, or discipline that you have practiced to help till the soil of your heart, to slow you down, and to allow your roots to go deeper into the things of God?

The Problem of Weeds and Thorns

Some soil is deep enough and soft enough, but it is just too cluttered for anything to grow. The soil is wasting its valuable nutrients on weeds! The seed is being choked out by the competition. Clutter sounds like such a small problem, but I would suggest that this is possibly the most dangerous soil condition of all. It is dangerous because it is so subtle.

Jesus talked a lot about the clutter and lure of wealth. We live in a world where we are bombarded with promises that the accumulation of things will make us happy. I once saw an advertisement for a car that went something like this, "You can't buy happiness . . . but now you can lease it!" There is a magazine called *The Good Life*. If you read all of the advertisements in this magazine you'd get the sense that the good life consists primarily of two things: fine dining and weight reduction. Talk about a formula that will lead to clutter in your life! You can eat too much, get in a car and drive too fast to a health club that costs too much, and then get on a bike that goes nowhere!

8. Take a moment to do a personal clutter assessment. What are a few of the things (they don't have to be bad things) that seem to be the weeds and thorns that fill the garden of your life?

   •
   •
   •

9. If you were going to do some weeding in your life, what is one easy and obvious weed you would need to pull?

What is one weed that might be a little tougher to pull, but still needs to go?

How can your small group members pray for you and keep you accountable as you do this weeding project in your life?

We Are the Seed and the Sowers

While God is working in our lives, part of our growth is learning that we are not only the soil, we are also called to be the sowers. Followers of Jesus Christ discover that they are called to scatter the seed of the Good News of Jesus Christ freely and generously. We need to sow the seed everywhere we go, because we never know what soil is prepared and ready.

Many of us have worked, prayed, loved, and scattered seed faithfully, yet we have not seen the harvest we would have wanted. We have reached out to family or friends and invited them to church or shared our testimony or even had a chance to tell them the story of God's love given in Jesus Christ. But, as far as we can tell, nothing seems to be happening. In time, a part of us starts to think that either we did something wrong or that God is not keeping up His part of the deal.

This parable reminds us that not all soil is ready to receive God's seed. The sower can spread the seed freely, and the seed is ready to do its work, but not all of the soil is soft, deep, or free of weeds. Jesus wants us to remember that our part is only to sow the seed. Our job is not to make growth happen; only God can do that. We don't have to understand how it all works, we just need to sow the seed and let God do His work.

10. What is one way you have discovered that is natural for you to scatter seed and spread the message of Jesus Christ?

What is one way your small group can work together to scatter seed and let others know that God loves them?

Celebrating and Being Celebrated

There are times in all of our lives when we need to be honest and confess that our hearts have grown hard. If you are at that point, give God a little opening by offering the following humble and honest prayer: "God, whatever you need to do, I want you to plow up the hardness of my heart. Please do it! I want to be tenderhearted toward you, but I can't do it on my own. Come and break up the hard soil of my life."

Take a few minutes for silent prayers of confession. At the close of this time, the Holy Spirit might lead a few of your small group members to pray out loud and allow their confession of hard-heartedness to be heard by the other group members. This is very biblical (see James 5:16). If this happens, take time as a group to pray for God's healing hand in the life of any group member who is led to pray out loud. If no one feels prompted to pray out loud, simply have one group member close your time of silent prayer with an "Amen" when it seems appropriate.

Loving and Being Loved

One of the greatest acts of love we could ever express is to freely scatter the seed of the Good News of Jesus Christ. This saving message and the love of God can change lives forever. Identify one person in your life who has not yet received the grace of God through Jesus Christ. Commit yourself to pray for that person daily over the coming month. Pray for the soil of his or her heart to grow soft and receptive to the seed of the Gospel (the message and person of Jesus). Also, ask God to show you creative and effective ways to scatter the seed of the Gospel in this person's life.

Serving and Being Served

Sometimes God uses us to help till the soil of a hard-hearted person. Identify a person in your life who seems very hard to the things of God. Commit to extend one act of service for this person in the coming week. Bathe this action in prayer and ask God to use it as part of His process of softening the person's heart.

SESSION TWO

Overcoming Resentment

MATTHEW 20:1–16

We live in a world of insiders and outsiders. There are those who have and those who have not. Children learn at a young age what it means to be in a club, and the gut-wrenching feeling of knowing you are not welcome. When a young girl tries out for a sports team and makes it, she knows the exhilaration of being "on the team." And when a young man gives his best and runs for Student Council and receives the news that he did not get elected, he knows the deep pain of being on the outside. This continues on into adulthood in the marketplace and in social settings.

What is true today was also true two thousand years ago in Jesus' day. In the first century the vineyard was a common metaphor for the people of Israel. Throughout the Old Testament, this image was used to help God's people understand many lessons about themselves. Consider this example from Isaiah:

> I will sing for the one I love
> a song about his vineyard:
> My loved one had a vineyard
> on a fertile hillside. . . .
> The vineyard of the LORD Almighty
> is the house of Israel,
> and the men of Judah
> are the garden of his delight.
>
> —Isaiah 5:1, 7a

The parable we are going to study in this session may sound as if it is about a vineyard, but what it is really about is the family of God—about who is inside the family of God and who is outside. It is a parable that gives us a window into the heart of God, who wants everyone to know that they are invited to be on the inside of His family.

In a world of fences and membership cards there should be one place where the doors are wide open—the church! And there should be one family that is never a closed circle—the family of God. Jesus threw the doors wide open and made access possible for all of us! No place in all the earth should be more inviting and welcoming than the church of Jesus Christ, and no one should have wider arms than a Christian.

Making the Connection

1. Describe a time when you made the team, were invited in, or found yourself on the inside of a closed circle. If you can't think of an example, then describe a time when you did not make the cut, were excluded, or found yourself clearly on the outside of a closed circle. How did you feel?

Knowing and Being Known

Read Matthew 20:1–16

2. What is unusual about the landowner's hiring practices and compensation program in this parable?

How do the landowner's practices reflect the way God reaches out to lost people and invites them into His family?

3. In this parable there are five groups of workers who are hired and eventually payed. How do you feel the last group of workers (who had only worked one hour) felt about their compensation in relationship to how the first group of workers (who had worked for twelve hours) felt about their pay for the day of work?

The Poison of Performance-Based Christianity

The workers hired at the first hour of the day represent those in the church who operate on a performance-based approach to life and faith. This can happen to some who have spent a lifetime in the church (the vineyard). Because these people have avoided certain scandalous sins, they begin to feel that God is getting a pretty good deal with them. Instead of rejoicing at those who come in at the last minute, they can begin to have a grumbling, resentful, judgmental spirit.

Then there are those who have what we could call grace-based Christianity. These are the latecomers, those who have no contract and no guarantees. They are desperate, in need of anything and everything Jesus can offer them. Their whole relationship with God is based on trust. These people are seized by joy over their good fortune. They are humbled because God is so good to them. They marvel at the greatness of God's character, and are motivated to work in the vineyard out of profound gratitude to Him.

4. How can performance-based Christianity poison the heart of the person who is caught up in it?

How can performance-based Christianity poison the health and witness of a local church?

5. When a person is captured by grace-based Christianity and overwhelmed by God's goodness, how is this reflected in his or her daily life?

A Complaining Spirit

Sometimes those who have been in the church for a long time can adopt a joyless spirit. When this poison begins to run through their veins, they become joy-challenged. These people actually seek out other complainers in order to justify their sinful disposition. They become blind to the good things around them and, if they do happen to notice anything good, they fail to celebrate or praise those things. Instead, they obsess over bad things and want everyone else to see them and obsess with them. This kind of complaining, joyless spirit is deadly and can kill both a church and the heart of a follower of Christ.

The antidote to a complaining spirit is the discipline of noticing. We need to learn how to pay attention, to slow down and see what God has done and is doing all around us. Then we need to declare and celebrate where God is at work.

6. The workers who had put in a full day and got a full denarius (exactly what they were promised) grumbled and complained (v. 11). When you look at the story from where they stood, how might you sympathize with their frustration and complaining?

   How have you seen a grumbling spirit hurt the health and life of a church?

7. The antidote to a complaining and grumbling spirit is developing a thankful spirit through slowing down and noticing all of God's goodness. What can you do to slow down the pace of your life over the coming month so you can make space for thankfulness?

A Resentful Spirit

Another mark of performance-based Christianity is a resentful spirit. This occurs when we experience God as a strict taskmaster and not as a loving Father. Resentment grows when we feel we always have to do something to gain God's love and approval. Instead of feeling like a deeply loved child, we feel like a dutiful soldier or faithful servant. It becomes harder and harder to believe that God really loves us just for who we are. Even if we immerse ourselves in all sorts of activities and commitments as Christians, a resentful spirit keeps us from drinking deeply at the fountain of Christ and experiencing restoration for our soul.

The antidote for a resentful spirit is to receive God's love for us. We need to reflect deeply on all God has done to show His love. Resentment begins to die when our hearts are gripped by the overwhelming reality of God's love for us.

8. How did the resentful spirit of the first group of workers in this parable (v. 12) impact the way they saw the other workers? How can this same negative attitude infect the church today and keep us from reaching those outside the family of God?

9. Read 1 John 3:1–3 and 4:9–10. How can a deep and clear understanding of God's love for us help us overcome performance-based Christianity?

A Judgmental Spirit

The first group of workers in this parable were deeply upset because the landowner had treated those who came to work in the final hour of the day as equal with them. The laborers who put in a full day's work expressed their displeasure with these telling words, "You have made them equal to us" (v. 12). There is a judgmental spirit here. "I have worked so hard and they slip in under the wire and get all the blessing I deserve! Where is the fairness in that? I am sacrificing more. I am suffering more. I'm the one doing all the work."

The antidote to this kind of a spirit is remembering. We need to remember that we are all latecomers! None of us can sit in a place of judgment because we have all come into God's family (His vineyard) by grace. We also need to remember that God dispenses gifts, not wages. Even those who work all day receive only a gift. None of us gets paid according to merit—if we did, we would all end up in hell! How incredible it is to remember that, instead of punishment, God has shown us His great mercy and lavished us with His goodness.

Describe a time when you were amazed and overwhelmed with a deep personal sense of God's love for you and His affection toward you.

10. If you came into the family of God at a young age, how is this a reminder of God's grace in your life and His provision for you?

If you came into the family of God (the vineyard) late in life, how have you experienced God's grace through His open invitation?

Whether you came into the family of God early or late, how can the members of your small group work together to extend an open invitation to others to come and enter God's family?

Celebrating and Being Celebrated

Every day we are lavished with gifts of grace. Each breath of life, each morning we wake up, each smile someone gives, each greeting and word of encouragement are reminders of God's grace. When we see a flower blossoming in spring, when we pick up a Bible and feed on the Word of God, when we walk into church to the sound of worship music, we are receiving grace! Yet even though we are surrounded by the goodness of God, we oftentimes don't even notice it. We need to develop eyes that see, a heart that responds, and lips that give praise to God.

Take a moment to write down three or four gifts or blessings God has lavished on you:

-
-
-
-

Have members of your small group close your time together by offering short prayers thanking God for His goodness in their lives.

Loving and Being Loved

If you are going to effectively communicate the love of Jesus to others, you need to receive His love fully. Take fifteen minutes three or four times in the coming week and find a quiet place where you can sit down and meditate deeply on 1 John 3:1–3:

> How great is the love the Father has lavished on us, that we should be called children of God! And that is what we are! The reason the world does not know us is that it did not know him. Dear friends, now we are children of God, and what we will be has not yet been made known. But we know that when he appears, we shall be like him, for we shall see him as he is. Everyone who has this hope in him purifies himself, just as he is pure.

Take time to memorize this passage and let the truth of God's love sink deeply into your heart. As you memorize this passage, personalize it. Know that it is telling you who you are and how much the Father loves you. Ask God to overwhelm you with the height and depth and breadth of His love. Remember that spiritual giants are ordinary people who have come to understand that they are dearly loved by the Father. Pray that your understanding of God's love will overflow to others.

Serving and Being Served

The greatest act of service we could ever offer to another person is to clearly communicate the love of God and the grace of Jesus Christ. Make a list of a few people you know who are not yet followers of Christ:

-
-
-

Pray for each of these people each day until your group meets again. Use the prayer guide provided below to direct your time in prayer:

- Pray that your life would be so filled with love, joy, and grace that your friends will see Christ alive and at work in you.
- Pray that your church (all the people of God in your congregation) will have a growing heart to reach out to those who are not yet followers of Jesus Christ.
- Pray for your heart to be cleansed of any complaining, resentment, or judgmental attitude so that you are a clean vessel through which God can work.
- Pray that God will give you an opportunity to tell your story of faith or to talk about the Good News of God's love in Jesus Christ with each of the people on your prayer impact list.

SESSION THREE

Don't Wait Until It's Too Late

MATTHEW 25:1–13

Have you ever had a dream like this? You show up at school for a class you have been taking all semester long. As you walk into the room you suddenly realize that it is the day of a big test, but you forgot about it. You did not study and are hopelessly unprepared. You sit there and know you don't have a chance of passing.

There is a story about a college student who has an experience like this. He is taking a class on ornithology (the study of birds). It is a very difficult class and the professor is famous for being a pretty tough character. The student thinks he is prepared, but with this professor, you never really know.

The day of the class final, the student walks in only to find no blue books, no questions, no exam papers. Instead, there are twenty-five pictures of birds hanging on the walls. But they are a very specific kind of picture; they are photographs of birds' feet. The professor explains that the entire final exam is going to be very specific. The students will have to identify the species of each bird by recognizing their feet.

This student is in shock. He is outraged as he realizes he does not have a chance of passing this test. Finally, as the shock is wearing off, he speaks up. "This is too hard. I studied. I tried to prepare. But no one can pass a test like this!"

The professor responds, "Too bad, that's the final."

The student shoots back, "This is completely unfair and I refuse to take the final."

The professor then informs the student (and the entire class) in no uncertain terms that "you will take this final or I will fail you right now!"

The student says, "Then fail me!"

The professor says, "Young man, what is your name? You just flunked Ornithology 101!"

At which the young man looks at the professor, takes off his shoes, and says, "You tell me!"

Whether or not this story actually took place is not the point. It is a humorous but clear reminder that when you are a student it is wise to remember that the final always comes. The wise student does not wait until the last minute and then cram for the exam. Likewise, in life, our final moment might not be today or tomorrow, but it is coming . . . never doubt it. If we are wise, we will live as those who are ready.

Making the Connection

1. Describe a dream or fear you have experienced about being late or unprepared.

   Tell about a time when you thought you could wait "a little bit longer" and got caught unprepared.

Knowing and Being Known

Read Matthew 25:1–13

2. How were the two groups of virgins in this story similar and how were they different?

What consequences did the second group of virgins face because of this one difference?

3. If you had to give this parable a title that gets to the heart of the message Jesus is communicating, what would it be?

No-Regret Finances

How many of us have made a financial choice that we later regretted? The truth is, most of us have! Yet Jesus would have us look at finances from an eternal perspective. He wants us to ask, "How will this investment look to me the day I die?" Most investment counselors don't think about the scope of eternity. But we need to.

Due to the affluence of our society, we have many choices regarding how to spend our money. We need to strive to live in such a way that when we look back we won't have to say, "If only I had it to do over again, I would have invested so much more in the things that really matter!"

Read 2 Corinthians 9:6–11

4. The apostle Paul gives a vision for how a follower of Christ approaches finances. Describe how God wants to impact our *attitude* and our *actions* when it comes to sharing what we have.

5. How might a spiritual skeptic view a follower of Christ who takes this call to generosity seriously?

6. Take a moment to plot where you see yourself on the two graphs below:

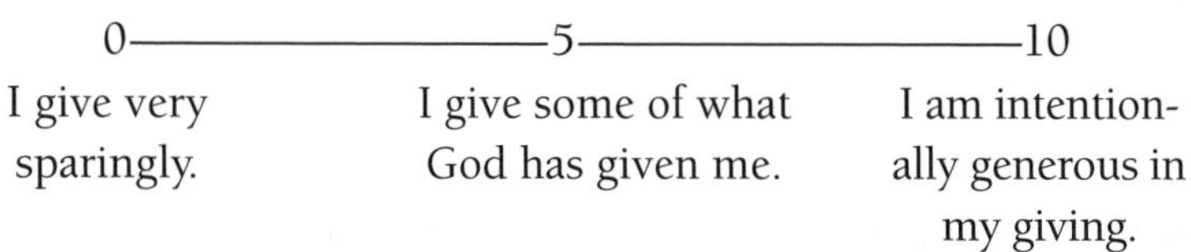

0——5——10

I give because I feel pressure but don't find joy in it.	I give and find some satisfaction in supporting God's work.	I find deep joy in giving and do it cheerfully.

What needs to happen in your life for you to take the next step in your giving and become more generous toward God and His work?

If you have had experiences when giving was joy-filled, describe what helped you grow as a cheerful giver.

No Regret When It Comes to Sin

Have you ever seen bad habits simply go away? You used to chew your nails, or call other drivers bad names, or lose your temper all the time. Then one day these behaviors simply disappear. You wake up and they are gone.

Of course not! That is just not the way bad habits work, and even less the way that sin works. Think back to the story of Cain in the Bible. Cain wanted to serve God, but his soul was poisoned with envy toward his brother. God said to Cain, "If you do what is right, will you not be accepted? But if you do not do what is right, sin is crouching at your door; it desires to have you, but you must master it" (Genesis 4:7).

Some of us need to identify the truth that sin is crouching at our door and that its desire is for us. If we simply quiet our hearts and ask God to show us, we will see danger areas such as bad habits, destructive patterns, abuse, addiction, racism, pride, judgment, chronic deceit, gossiping, dishonesty, sexual misbehavior, sharp-tongued sarcasm, attitudes that wither our spirit, and a host of other sins.

But we need not fall victim to the sins that lie in wait for us. We are not passive victims who have no way of escape. If we are committed to mounting a full-scale attack, by God's grace we can master the sinful habits in our lives.

Read Genesis 4:6–16

7. What was God's warning to Cain about the temptation of sin and how did Cain respond to this warning?

What are some of the ways God seeks to warn us about the potential consequences of our sins?

8. What were some of the consequences of Cain's decision to do things his way instead of God's way?

What is one consequence you have faced in your life because you decided to follow the enticement of sin and not the warnings of God?

9. One of the best deterrents to sin is honestly looking at what we might regret later. As a group, choose one of the scenarios below and seek to list some of the possible consequences or regrets in the life of a person who chooses to follow the path of sin and not the counsel of God:

   - A person in the workplace who is tempted to "borrow" supplies and small sums of money he feels no one will ever notice are gone.

   - A married person who is feeling enticed to pursue a friendship and one-on-one time with a person of the opposite sex toward whom he or she feels a strong attraction.

   - A person who has a growing need for alcohol to carry him or her through the day.

No Regret When It Comes to Taking Risks

God calls all of His followers to be willing to take some risks for His sake. The nation of Israel is a classic example of a people who failed to take risks. God called the Israelites to go into the Promised Land and take it in His power. But even after having witnessed the Passover and God's mighty deliverance from Egypt through the parting of the Red Sea, the Israelites were not willing to put their trust in God. They were literally standing on the edge of God's promise and all they had to do was take a step and cross over, but they refused because of their fear. They would not take the risk. Many of them went to their graves never having stepped foot on the Promised Land.

Read Numbers 13:1–2, 26–33; 14:6–9

10. Twelve men went into the Promised Land to investigate what it was like. Describe the report and attitude of the ten who were opposed to entering the land and also the attitude of the two who wanted to enter the land.

    The negative report had significant impact on the whole nation of Israel. What regrets do you think the nation of Israel had about not taking the risk and entering the land?

11. What is one risk you feel God might want you to take that you have been resisting? How can your small group members pray for you and encourage you to step out in faith and take this risk?

Celebrating and Being Celebrated

One key to growing in generosity is being clear about all of the good things God has poured out on your life. When we see His generosity, we become more free to give. Take a moment to write down several of the material blessings God has given you.

God has given me:

-
-
-

Loving and Being Loved

God has revealed His love for us by sending His Son to die on a cross and pay for our sins. He calls us to respond in love by repenting of sin and turning from ongoing sinful practices. Take time in the coming days to show your love for God by identifying one area in your life in which you are facing ongoing temptation. Follow the process below as you seek to express your love for God and walk in His ways:

1. Identify a very specific area you are facing temptation:

   ____

2. Confess this area of temptation to God and ask Him to fill you with the power of His Holy Spirit to resist temptation.
3. Write down some of the very real and specific consequences you might face if you continue to walk in the way of sin and not to follow the leading of God in this area:

   Consequences I might face . . .

   -
   -
   -

4. Invite one close Christian friend to pray for you and keep you accountable to honor God in this area of your life.

Serving and Being Served

We are called to be cheerful givers. Consider a radical act of service in the coming month. Pray about one possession you have that you feel God might want you to give up. Sell this item and give the resources to your church or some mission organization. Be sure to pray for God to give you a joyous spirit in this adventure of giving. Let this be a first step in your life toward no-regret finances.

SESSION FOUR

An Invitation to Return Home

LUKE 15:11–24

In our lives, we choose daily between two alternatives: We either choose to live at home with the Father or away in a distant land. When we are at home with the Father we invite God to be with us all day. We know that we can be in constant communication with Him, so we ask Him to get rid of any thoughts that don't please Him. We know that our primary identity is that we are His beloved children, so we are not easily threatened or made anxious. We know that we are perfectly safe in His hands, so we are not easily discouraged by problems and challenges. God's deepest desire is for us to live at home with Him and walk in this peace.

But there is another way to live. In the language of the passage we will study today it is "to be in a distant country." When we live in a distant country we don't often think of God. To be reminded of Him just makes us feel guilty for some of the choices we have made. Sins like deceit or gossip become increasingly attractive. We no longer have an inner sense of freedom, but instead feel weighed down because we know something is wrong. When we are in this "distant country" we feel hurried, rushed, easily irritated, and often threatened. We search for bursts of pleasure, but cannot find sustained joy.

Making the Connection

1. Describe how you have felt when you have been close to the Father and had your feet planted firmly at home.

Describe how you have felt when you have wandered to a distant land.

Knowing and Being Known

Read Luke 15:11–24

2. What decisions did the son make and what attitudes did he display that led him to a pig's trough?

   What decisions did he make and what attitude changes occurred to lead him back to his father?

3. What do you learn about the heart and character of the father in this story?

Crossroad #1—Temptation

For the prodigal, the temptation stage was reached before the story begins. Somewhere along the line a thought occurred to him, "Living at home is a burden. I would be happier away from my father and without all these constraints in my life."

We see this in kids sometimes. Some children are very compliant and love to be home with their parents. Others are not nearly as compliant and pose much more of a challenge.

James Dobson writes about a two-year-old named Frankie who was a noncompliant child. He tells how Frankie pulled a chair over to the front window and carefully placed it inside the drapes. He was standing there looking out at the world beyond his window when his mother came looking for him. She saw his little white legs protruding beneath the drapes and quietly slipped in behind him. Then she heard her two-year-old little boy speaking to himself in very sober terms. He was saying, "I gotta get out of here."

In this parable we meet a young man who is saying, "I gotta get out of here! Here at home I always have to do what father says. I have to work in his fields, eat at his table, follow his rules. I don't want to have to do this anymore. My life would be better if I had no rules. I could be my own boss, I could chart my own course. I gotta get out of here!"

4. Describe a time when you faced temptation, considered the consequences, and said no. When you look back, why are you glad you made the right choice? What might it have cost you had you entered into this area of temptation?

5. Describe a time when you faced temptation and entered in. What do you wish you had done differently? Describe the cost you and others paid because of this decision to live outside of the Father's will.

Crossroad #2—Action

This huge step moves us from considering and thinking about a temptation to pursuing a sinful course of action. For the prodigal son this step occurred when he went to his father and asked for his inheritance. He had convinced himself that he had a right to his father's property. In truth, the property rightfully belonged to his father, both legally and ethically.

If most people toy around with the idea of sin long enough, they will eventually move into action. Whatever the sin, the movement from thought to action always happens at the same point: when the person finds an acceptable rationale or pretext to do it. Rationalizing is universal among fallen people. Some people say, "It's just a harmless conversation or flirtation," when they know an unhealthy attraction is growing. Others rationalize by saying to themselves, "The company does not pay me enough, and I work a lot of extra hours," as they pad expense accounts and begin to steal from the company. If you see yourself rationalizing a behavior, watch out! Are you about to take the giant step from temptation into action that James warns us about (James 1:14–16)?

6. When you have faced temptation in the past, what has helped you stand strong and resist it?

7. Describe the end results of the son's decisions and how these are like the end results of our actions when we choose to leave the Father.

8. Identify one area in your life in which you are standing at a crossroad that will take you from temptation to action. How can your small group members pray for you and challenge you to resist the temptation and not enter into this action that will take you away from the Father?

Crossroad #3—Pain

Some time ago I was about to have surgery on my knee. When I asked the doctor what I could expect after the surgery, he answered in one word, "Pain." He informed me that there would be two primary ways I could deal with the pain. The first way would be to take some pills that would not deal with the source of the problem but would mask the pain for a little while. The second way to deal with the pain would be to face it. He then warned me that the pills would last for only a short while and then I would have to begin rehabilitation and deliberately experience pain in order to build up my body and be well and whole again.

In my first rehab session after surgery I had one of the most sensitive and tender therapists I could imagine. Each time she asked me to make any movement she would ask if I was feeling pain. If I said yes or she thought I looked like I was experiencing any discomfort, she would stop. There was not much pain, *but there was also not much progress.*

For my next session I got a physical therapist with a radically different approach to therapy. She was a solid, strong woman who was ferociously committed to my long-term health and wellness. She had me lay on my stomach and then she grabbed the foot on my injured leg and bent it back as far as her heavily muscled arms could bend it. I said, "I'm feeling some pain." She responded with an enthusiastic, "Yes! Feel the pain! Embrace the pain! The pain is our friend!" It was a whole different session in terms of pain, *but we made amazing progress.*

9. In this parable the son finally hits the wall of pain (vv. 14–16). Describe the son's response to his pain in *one* of the following areas:

—How he viewed himself

—How he viewed his father

—How he viewed his future

10. How has God used the crossroad of pain in your life to bring you back into His arms?

Crossroad #4—Living As a Child of God or a Hired Servant

Once the son hits the crossroad of pain, he has to make a decision. Will he continue to live in ever-increasing levels of pain away from the father or will he humble himself and go home? The pain wakes him up and he is finally ready to go back to the father. But as he prepares himself, he also reveals his own sense of unworthiness. He writes a little speech that he is ready to give to his father when he arrives home (vv. 18–19). In this speech he reveals the fact that he no longer sees himself as a beloved son of the father, but worthy only of the status of a hired servant.

As a hired servant he will be a free man with his own income and will live in the village. He can keep a certain level of autonomy. He might be able to pay the father back some of what he has squandered and may even be able to render helpful services. However, he will never again know the intimacy of a son with a father. He will never again feel the warmth and tenderness of knowing a father is looking on him with favor and joy.

But the father has a whole different plan in mind!

11. What contrast do you see between how the son sees himself and how the father sees him (vv. 17–24)?

12. This parable reveals the heart of the Father toward you. How would you describe the disposition of God's heart toward you today?

Celebrating and Being Celebrated

Close your session with a time of prayer thanking God for treating you as beloved daughters and sons. Give Him praise that He does not put you on probation as hired servants, but that His arms and home are always open.

Loving and Being Loved

Take time in the coming weeks to read and reflect deeply on Hebrews 12:4–13. Examine your own personal history and the times God has brought the loving pain of discipline to your life. Take time in prayer to thank Him for loving you enough to discipline you.

Serving and Being Served

The truth of God's unyielding fatherly affection is life-changing. Commit to writing a note to one or two friends who are followers of Christ reminding them that they are beloved children of the Father. Communicate what you have learned from this session and let them know that you felt prompted to remind them of one of the greatest truths in all the world . . . they are a beloved child of God.

SESSION FIVE

Heart-Healing Forgiveness

LUKE 7:36–50

In every culture various kinds of etiquette surround many aspects of life. Mealtime etiquette is certainly one of these areas. In some cultures it is considered a compliment to belch after a meal; in other cultures this is seen as quite rude. For some people, elbows on the table can be seen as offensive. There are rules for setting a table, for who gets served first, for conversation, and for what to do after a meal. Consider a couple of the following situations. What do you think is the proper behavior based on rules of etiquette?

When should one start eating the main course at a formal dinner?

A. After the hostess is served.
B. After the hostess lifts her fork.
C. After three or four people are served.
D. A.S.A.P. with urgency and passion.

When should the hostess be served first?

A. Never.
B. If it's her birthday.
C. If the first portion is hard to extract.
D. If she's a greedy pig.

The answers to these questions (according to Emily Post, an etiquette expert) are found in the leader's notes in the back of this study guide.

Rules of etiquette help govern how we behave in social settings. No one is thrown in jail for breaking these rules, but they can impact how people feel. Following them can affirm a person and breaking them can be very insulting.

Making the Connection

1. What are some commonly accepted rules of etiquette in our culture?

Tell a story about a time when you broke a rule of etiquette.

Knowing and Being Known

Read Luke 7:36–39, 40–47

Breaking All the Rules

In this passage, we need to notice the gross neglect when Jesus came to this home as a visiting rabbi. There was no kiss of greeting, no washing of the feet, no anointing with oil. These were not subtle omissions easily overlooked. Simon was breaking every rule of etiquette when it came to having an honored guest in his home. Jesus was ignored and insulted, and every indication is that it was quite deliberate . . . an intentional slap in the face. Every one of the guests would have felt the tension in the room.

Into this scene a woman enters. Luke gives us some very specific information about this woman. She was "a sinner" (v. 37). From the Greek word Luke uses, it is quite clear that she was a very specific kind of sinner, a prostitute. This is a woman who wouldn't have been invited to a dinner like this in a million years, yet she approaches the table. Jesus and the other guests would have been reclining at the table with their feet extended away from it. Now it is the woman's turn to break a whole different set of rules of etiquette.

Simon had not greeted Jesus with a kiss, but this woman lavishes Jesus with kisses on His feet. Jesus' feet were still dirty from the dusty streets as no one had offered to wash them when He entered the banquet. The woman begins to wash His feet with her tears and dry them with her hair. Simon had not offered oil for anointing when Jesus entered, but this sinful woman pours out all she has from the perfume flask she wore around her neck.

2. Imagine you were a guest at the table and you had watched Simon's conduct at this dinner. How might you have felt toward him?

   How might you have felt toward the woman and her breaches of etiquette?

3. What does Simon's etiquette-breaking neglect teach you about the condition of his heart?

   What do the woman's etiquette-breaking actions teach you about the condition of her heart?

4. Look at this parable as a mirror reflecting the condition of your heart. How do you see yourself reflected as you look at each of these rule breakers?

A Story of Two Debtors

In Jesus' day people called moneylenders would offer to help people out of a jam by loaning them money at very high interest rates. In those days, people who allowed themselves to get into debt were not highly thought of. And those who would lend out money at interest were seen as an even worse class of people. They were shady characters. In our day this story would begin, "Let me tell you about two bookies who were in over their heads to a loan shark called Big Louie."

In this story, both debtors owe money and neither of them can pay it back. Both men face the same fate. The only difference is that while one of the debts looks manageable and the debtor carries the illusion that maybe there is a way out, the other guy knows he is desperate. The truth is, both of these debtors could expect to lose all they had and had only prison or worse to look forward to. Just then the loan shark calls them in and says, "I'm going to make you an offer you can't refuse" and both debts are forgiven.

Jesus then asks Simon and the people at the table which of these two debtors was going to have his world turned upside down. Which one would be filled with relief, gratitude, and joy? Which would be seized by love for the one who forgave his debt? Jesus poses a very simple question to Simon, "Which of them will love him more?" Simon sees where this is headed, but all eyes are on him so he has to answer. He says, "I *suppose* the one who had the bigger debt." Jesus says—I think with a little humor—"You have judged correctly!"

Read Luke 7:40–43

5. In this story Jesus uses the two debtors to represent the Pharisee, Simon, and the sinful woman. As you look at this entire passage, what do these two people have in common and how are they different?

6. Jesus is deeply concerned about the sins of pride and self-righteousness. What are some of the warning signs that spiritual pride is growing in a person's heart and life?

7. Jesus longs for us to come to Him in genuine humility, aware of our sin and need for His grace. What has helped you grow in humility and clarify your perspective on who you are in relationship to Jesus?

Everything Put in Perspective

Now the drama changes significantly. Up to this point Jesus has been interacting with Simon, but now Jesus turns toward the woman, who is on the ground behind Him. This would mean that Jesus had to, in effect, turn His attention away from Simon and all the guests at the table. Jesus faces the woman, but as He does, He continues to talk to Simon.

He asks Simon if he has seen the woman. Well, of course he has—everyone has seen her. Yet Simon had seen only a theological object lesson or a focal point for his contempt. He had not seen what Jesus saw—no one had. At this moment Jesus makes a gracious but powerful series of declarations. He reminds Simon that he had not provided foot washing but that this woman had used her own tears to wash His feet and her own hair to dry them. Jesus points out Simon's failure to give a kiss of greeting, and celebrates this woman's lavish freedom with kissing His feet. Then Jesus reminds Simon, and everyone around the table, that he had not been offered oil for His head, but this woman had poured out precious perfume on His feet. Jesus announces to everyone gathered around the table, and to anyone else who is in earshot, that this woman is the one who has been forgiven much and who has loved much.

Now Simon has to figure out how he fits into the parable Jesus had told just minutes earlier. If this woman was the one who was forgiven much and who loved much, who was Simon?

Read Luke 7:44–50

8. Imagine yourself back at the table as a guest at this banquet. Jesus, the visiting rabbi, has just spoken these powerful words to Simon, host of the banquet. As you look around the room, describe what you think is going through the mind of *one* of the following people:

   —Simon

   —The sinful woman

   —Jesus

   —Yourself as one of the guests

9. Describe the last time you found yourself at the feet of Jesus in deep worship, amazed at His grace and celebrating His love.

10. What can you do in your schedule and personal disciplines to deepen as a worshiper and make more time to be at the feet of the Savior?

Celebrating and Being Celebrated

As your group closes in prayer, move in two very distinct directions. First, take time for confession (either silent or out loud). Confess sins of self-righteousness and pride. Confess any sense of feeling that you deserve God's grace on your own merit.

Second, take time for humble adoration. Spend some moments at the feet of Jesus as a small group. If your meeting space allows, you might even want to invite group members to kneel, if they feel comfortable doing so. Pour out the perfume of your worship and bathe the feet of Jesus with the kisses of your love. Take time as a group to let the Savior know you are overwhelmed by His love and amazed by His grace.

Loving and Being Loved

In this story we meet a religious leader who has come to a place of exalting himself and looking down on others, especially sinners. He has forgotten that he is just as sinful as this woman and, in some ways, maybe more sinful. In his mind, she is an outsider, undesirable. Yet Jesus taught that anyone is welcome at His table if they come as one who loves and worships Him.

This story raises the question, "Who is really the big debtor?" Everyone could see that there was great sin at that banquet table, but it was not the sin that Simon thought it was. It was the sin of lips that wouldn't kiss, knees that wouldn't kneel, eyes that wouldn't weep, and hands that wouldn't serve.

It was the sin of perfume that would never leave the jar, the sin of a heart that would not break, a life that would not change, and a soul too stubborn and proud to love.

Take time in the coming weeks to ask the Holy Spirit to reveal any prejudice or pride in your life when it comes to who you believe is welcome in the church. Sometimes there are certain individuals or groups of people we would rather not see show up at our church or in our fellowship. If God brings to your heart anyone you have judged as unworthy of His grace and unwelcome among His people, commit yourself to praying for three things in the coming days:

1. Pray for a broken spirit and a humble heart so that you can see yourself as needing grace just as much as this person does.
2. Pray for the Lord to work in this person's heart and soften him or her toward the things God has to offer.
3. Pray for God to use you to extend love and grace to this person in some practical way in the coming week. In addition, pray for an opportunity to invite him or her to visit your church or even to your home for a meal.

Serving and Being Served

Sometimes our service is rendered to those in need; at other times it is extended to those who are part of our church community. In this story, the service is being offered humbly to Jesus not by the religious leader, but by the sinful woman. In the story, she takes what is most precious to her and pours it on Jesus' feet. Take time in the coming week to reflect deeply on your own commitment to worship Jesus with all your heart. Are you giving Him your best and laying it at His feet? Do you worship passionately, give generously, sing joyfully, and learn humbly? Over the coming month, seek to take deeper steps in serving Jesus by going deeper as His worshiper.

SESSION SIX

Spiritual Sincerity

MATTHEW 21:28–32

A story in two acts.

In the first act we meet a family sitting around the breakfast table: a father, a mother, and two grown sons. Both boys work on the family farm. Dad tells son number one to go work the back forty. This first son is a bit surly and strong-willed. On top of that, he is not above mouthing-off to Dad and being outright stubborn. He wears ripped jeans, a T-shirt, and has a pack of cigarettes in his sleeve. He looks up from his Pop Tart and says, "Me? The back forty? Long hours, minimum pay, back-breaking labor? I don't think so!" He gets up from the table and tells his dad, "It's not going to fit into my schedule today!" He walks out of the house, jumps on his Harley, and heads off to see his heavily-tattooed, body-pierced girlfriend.

The father turns toward his other son. This son is wearing khaki pants, a button-down oxford shirt and is eating a bowl full of Wheaties.

Have you ever noticed that when one child is misbehaving, another one will get so sweet? When the father gives the same command to this son, he is cheerful and compliant. He goes so far as to say, "I'll go, sir!" which is exactly what his father wants to hear. The second boy is the good boy, the helpful child, the shining light in his father's galaxy . . . at least for the moment.

This second son reminds me of a character from the old show *Leave It to Beaver*. Eddie Haskel was a friend of Wally Cleaver who was always giving compliments and buttering up every adult who crossed his path, but as soon as they were gone his true colors came out. This second son is a modern-day Eddie Haskel. He says, "The back forty? Sure, Dad! It would be an honor for me. Maybe there are some who don't appreciate such a great opportunity to work, but I would love to spend the day out there working for you. What a privilege to serve! As a matter of fact, just this morning, during my rather lengthy time of prayer and Scripture reading I was actually thinking how much I love to work in the back forty." You get the point. There is a phony willingness to his enthusiasm.

Dad and Mom look at their model son and think how proud they are to have such a willing, helpful, and cooperative child. He is the hero of the breakfast table. But remember, this is only the first act of the drama. There is more to come.

In the second act, the tough and resistant son gets on his Harley and begins driving, but something happens. He can't get his father's words out of his mind. As he is riding away he begins thinking of his father and all he has done for him over the years. With time, his heart softens and he hits the brakes. He makes a U-turn on his Harley, heads back home, and drives out to the back forty. When he gets there he picks up his tools and starts to work. A moment later his father comes around the corner. To his surprise, he sees his tough, resistant son hard at work.

The father also notices something else as the morning passes: His cheerful, willing, enthusiastic son has not shown up. The day passes and his compliant, Eddie Haskel-like son never comes out to share in the labor. The father begins to figure out that this son who promised to be out in the field sharing the load never intended to come at all.

Making the Connection

1. Describe a time you met a person who was like the second son in an Eddie Haskel sort of way. How do you feel when you are around people like this?

Read Matthew 21:28–32

The God of the Dinner Table

In writing about this parable, pastor Earl Palmer gives some very valuable insight. About the first son he says, "The first son might be described as a big problem at the breakfast table but a great joy at dinner time." Later he makes this observation, "The second son was a joy at breakfast but a big problem at supper." What we have to understand is that this parable is a parable about dinner time! That's what really matters.

Like the first son, we need to face the reality that it is tough to follow the calling of Jesus Christ. We all have moments in which we have to admit that we struggle. None of us has an easy road when it comes to walking and growing in holiness. It reminds me of a prayer I once heard:

Dear Lord, so far today I am doing all right. I have not gossiped, lost my temper, been greedy, grumpy, nasty, selfish, or overindulgent. However, in a few minutes I will be getting out of bed. Then I will need a lot more help after that, Amen!

We all need help as we seek to honor the Father by saying yes and then living out this commitment with sincerity.

2. What do you learn about the heart of each son as you read the parable?

3. After finishing this short parable, Jesus compares the first son to one group of people and the second son to another group (vv. 31–32). What comparisons does Jesus make?

4. Take a moment to write down or identify one area in your life in which you are facing spiritual insincerity. Identify an area in which you might be outwardly saying yes to God, but your life is not supporting your words. If you feel comfortable doing so, tell your group about this area of struggle.

Step #1 toward Spiritual Sincerity ... Confrontation

As Jesus is applying this story, He reminds His listeners that John the Baptist came in the way of righteousness and confronted people. People came to John the Baptist to be baptized as a sign of repentance because they were aware of their sinfulness. But the religious leaders defied John, who greeted them with the words, "You brood of vipers." This is the ministry of confrontation. John's words were not designed to ingratiate him to these religious leaders. He told them they needed to bear fruit that was worthy of repentance. He let them know they needed to change, repent, turn around, and go the other way.

Later on, John the Baptist ministered in the same way to King Herod, who was governor over Israel. Herod had taken his own sister-in-law away from his brother to be his own wife. John was the only one who confronted him on this. He told him that what he was doing was wrong in God's eyes and that it would lead to judgment.

Herod lived with a strange tension. He respected John and liked to listen to him teach, yet at the same time he feared John and was troubled by his teaching. In the gospel of Mark we learn that Herod knew John was a righteous and holy man. He also realized that his own life was out of line, but a part of him resisted this confrontation. Sadly, Herod ended up ordering John's execution after being manipulated and tricked by Herodias.

5. There are times when God needs to confront us and wake us up to our need for repentance and change in our lives. Tell about a time when God confronted you through *one* of the following avenues:
   - Through the conviction of His Word, the Bible
   - Through the Spirit working in your heart in a time of corporate worship
   - Through the words of an unbeliever
   - Through a trusted brother or sister in Christ
   - Through some other means

6. Think of someone in your life who loves Jesus deeply and whom you trust enough to let him or her speak words of confrontation and conviction into your life. Describe how God uses this person in your life and you in this person's life.

Step #2 toward Spiritual Sincerity . . . Response

We are in danger when we become like the second son in this parable, when we give insincere and superficial compliance. This is when we claim to want to do the Father's will and smile as we say yes, but know that we have no intention of living it out. The second son's compliance and words of agreement were only a device to avoid confrontation and pain. We need to be careful that this is not happening in our spiritual lives.

I am thinking of the Christian who comes to church and sings, "Have your own way, Lord. Have your own way," at the top of his voice. He continues, "You are the Potter, I am the clay," but if anyone in his house tries to get the remote control out of his hand, the clay will get pretty hard. For people like this, the number one tactic is confrontation avoidance. Growth will never happen in our lives until we value facing truth more than avoiding pain.

When we are ready to face the truth and live with the pain, we enter the point of response. This is when we say, "God, I see my insincerity and my fear of confrontation. I am ready to face it, with Your strength. Give me the courage and power I need to respond to Your loving confrontation. Lord, I am ready to change."

7. Once we have been confronted with the truth, we can resist or respond. Tell about a time you were confronted by the truth and responded in a way that brought you back into the vineyard of the Father.

8. Earlier in this session you wrote down a very specific area in which you feel you might be facing spiritual insincerity. What might be standing in the way of your responding to God's leading toward repentance in this area?

How can your small group members pray for you and help you over these hurdles?

Step #3 toward Spiritual Sincerity . . . Transformation

When we look at the ministry of Jesus we begin to realize that He was a genius at the process of bringing about spiritual transformation. He confronts us with the truth about ourselves, elicits a response, and then calls us into an ongoing process of transformation.

Think of Jesus' relationship with the tax collector Zacchaeus. It is pretty clear which of the seven deadly sins had a grip on his life—greed. So Jesus comes to the tree where Zacchaeus is hiding and confronts him and tells him the truth about himself. Zacchaeus invites Jesus to his home and, by Christ's grace, Zacchaeus is immediately changed. This transformed lifestyle becomes the antidote to greed! He goes on to pay back everyone four times what he overtaxed them. After that, he gives away half of his wealth. Can you see how this disciplined plan of giving might change Zacchaeus' addiction to the wealth of this world? Disciplined actions that bring us into compliance to the will of the Father radically transform our lives.

9. This parable is about the comparison of words and actions. One son says no, but goes to work in the fields. The other says yes, but never shows up. What would you say to a person who makes this claim: "I am truly sorry about a specific sin in my life. I have asked for forgiveness and I feel really bad about it. But I have no intention of stopping. I will continue in this sin."

10. Go back to your area of spiritual insincerity. What transformation and change needs to happen in your life for you to be walking in spiritual sincerity and to be living a life where you are in the vineyard and obeying the Father?

How can your small group members keep you accountable to seek this kind of transformation in the coming days?

Celebrating and Being Celebrated

Close your session by praying for God to fill you with a hunger for spiritual sincerity. Pray for real transformation to happen in the lives of each group member. If you have communicated specific areas in which you desire to grow, be sure to pray for each other.

Loving and Being Loved

As you have walked through this study as a small group there has been some honest confession and some deep vulnerability. Some group members have disclosed areas in which they feel God is calling them to a deeper place of spiritual sincerity. Take time in the coming week to contact one of your group members and let him know you respect him and commit to pray for and encourage him as he grows in this area of his life.

Serving and Being Served

Transformation takes time and deep commitment. It involves developing new disciplines and inviting the Spirit to bring change over time. If you have identified an area in which you feel called to grow in spiritual sincerity, humbly pray about one person that might be able to support you and help you grow in this area. It might be a person who has modeled maturity in this area of his or her life over time. Allow this person to serve you by communicating your sense of call to grow in this area and by asking him or her to pray for you and to help you grow in this area.

Session One – Overcoming Growth Barriers

MATTHEW 13:3–23

Question 1

Some would say that this is the premier parable of them all. It appears in the gospels of Matthew, Mark and Luke. It is an extended parable that is followed by Jesus giving very specific teaching and commentary on the meaning of the story. Along with this, the parable gets to the heart of one of the most important issues of life and faith.

This is a parable about growth. God's intention for His Kingdom and for all human beings is for them to thrive. The parable addresses God's heart on this topic of growth and also helps to reveal some of the primary barriers that can keep us from thriving. While the primary reading of the text addresses the barriers that stand in the way of a person first coming to a place of faith in God, these barriers can also stunt continued growth in the life of a follower of Christ. In this session we will look at barriers from both of these vantage points and ask the question, "How can followers of Christ grow in their faith and continue to thrive each and every day?"

Growth is the normative condition of living things. As long as we live we are growing, gaining new skills, and mastering new tasks. When we cease growing, we start dying. There is no greater tragedy than stagnation. As Jesus looked around, He saw people whose lives were choked by anger, whose hearts were paralyzed by fear, whose hopes were suffocated by doubt. Jesus said, with a broken heart, "Failure to thrive . . . failure to thrive."

As Jesus began to teach, we note that Matthew gives some very specific information. He tells us that Jesus sat down. First Jesus sat on the shore of the lake, and then He sat in a boat. Why does this matter? Because in those days, sitting was the formal posture that indicated teaching was going to begin. Even to this day, in many synagogues there is a chair in the front where the rabbi will sit when the teaching begins. Jesus sat down to let everyone know that it was time to learn. May you be open to learning from the Master Rabbi as you study this parable.

Questions 2–3

This story has three elements: a sower, seed, and soil. This is one of those parables where you need to look at the elements in the story and take note of what stays constant and what changes. When you identify the variable in the story, you begin to understand what Jesus wants us to see.

In this story, we can see that the seed does not change. This is not a story about good seed and bad seed. The seed, the Word of God, the Good News, will always bear fruit if you give it half a chance. Also, the sower does not change. This is not a story about good sowers and bad sowers. As a matter of fact, the sower is extravagant. He does not seem to be very concerned about where the seed lands, he just spreads it everywhere.

If the seed does not change and the sower does not change, then what is the variable? It is the soil. The soil has a direct impact on whether or not the seed can take root and begin to grow and thrive. Everything hinges on the soil. The soil, of course, represents human beings . . . us! When we talk about the condition of the soil, we can replace the word "soil" with "our hearts and lives." Although growth is normal, there are many kinds of soil that can keep the seed from growing.

In this session we are going to do a little soil analysis. We are going to look at our hearts and lives and ask if there are any barriers to growth within us. Are there some things that need to change?

Questions 4–5

One of the reasons Jesus spoke in parables is that He knew how hard-hearted people can be. Once, when the disciples asked Jesus why He spoke in parables, He quoted from Isaiah and said:

> This is why I speak to them in parables:
> "Though seeing, they do not see;
> though hearing, they do not hear or understand."
> In them is fulfilled the prophecy of Isaiah:

'You will be ever hearing but never understanding;
you will be ever seeing but never perceiving.
For this people's heart has become calloused;
they hardly hear with their ears,
and they have closed their eyes.
Otherwise they might see with their eyes,
hear with their ears,
understand with their hearts
and turn, and I would heal them.'"

—Matthew 13:13–15

In other words, people resist the truth. They can see, but they don't want to see. They can hear, but they don't want to hear. They have set up defenses to keep out the truth and the voice of God. But Jesus knew that stories could reach people even when their defenses were up. It was as if Jesus were flying in under their radar and bringing the truth of God through a story. Jesus wants to do some surgery on our hearts, but like most people, we do not want Him to cut through the hardness.

Questions 6–7

Many people have been hurt by painful relationships. They are holding on to bitterness and resentment. These people need to ask God to make their heart tender again. They need to go to the person who has hurt them and prayerfully say whatever they need to say to heal the relationship and make things right.

Others may have had dreams that crumbled and were never fulfilled, or hopes that were never realized. With time, a shell forms around their heart and they become cynical. They believe the worst about others. They are suspicious and void of any spirit of gratitude alive in their heart. The soil of their heart needs to be plowed.

My guess is that if soil had feelings, it would not want to be plowed, because plowing hurts! Breaking up hard ground is a painful process. But this is not the worst pain. The worst pain is to remain hard, barren, without fruit.

There is good news for hard soil: all it takes is a small opening. Just give the seed a crack. The seed is strong beyond our wildest imagination. Have you ever seen a little crack in a sidewalk with a blade of something forcing its way up through a concrete sidewalk? The seed, the Word of God, is powerful beyond what we can imagine. If we can find just a little place of soft soil and spread the seed, stand back and watch what God can do.

Questions 8–9

Jesus says that where there is clutter, all you will have is a weed patch. It is time for some of us to do some weeding. Now, here is the thing about weeds. Rarely do they go away on their own. Weeds don't just say, "We've been in this yard long enough, let's go visit another yard." As a matter of fact, they get worse with time and take over territory. By their very nature, they spread.

Some of us need to weed clutter out of our lives. Maybe the weed of workaholism is choking the spiritual life out of you. You might need to cut back on the hours you spend at work. Maybe being financially overextended is choking the spiritual joy of generosity right out of your life. You might need to do some financial weeding. You might be dramatically overextended in your family life. Between school and community opportunities, your children are signed up for so many things that they never get a break. You have become their personal taxi service, and the meter is always running. You might need to declare one or two nights a week as off limits for anything but down time with the family. You might need to say one sport at a time, or only one activity club at a time. Help your family learn how to weed out some of the clutter that has accumulated in your lives.

Jesus says, "Where the soil is soft, deep, and uncluttered, watch and see what can happen!" It is absolutely amazing what God can do in the life of one whose heart is ready to receive all He wants to give. If your heart is tender toward God, your devotion is deep and rooted, and your life is uncluttered, growth can't be stopped. You will thrive.

The people in Jesus' day had a sense of what it meant to thrive. They lived in an agricultural setting where they knew the joy of a good harvest. In those days, one good seed would produce a stalk and a head of grain. In a good year you might get a yield of twenty or twenty-five heads. But then Jesus begins talking about what the Father wants to do in the lives of those whose hearts are open and who are ready to thrive. He speaks of a harvest of thirty, or sixty, or even a hundredfold—far beyond what anyone could imagine. The point Jesus is making is that the fruitfulness God desires and expects in the lives of His people is beyond human comprehension or ability.

Question 10

One reason Jesus told this story was to encourage His followers. As His followers we are not just the soil, we are also called to be sowers. We are given the privilege of sowing seed. And while not all the seed we scatter will bear fruit, when the seed hits receptive soil, just watch what happens, though it is not our job to change people; only God can do that. However, as the soil of our hearts grows soft, we will grow in our enthusiasm to scatter the seed of God's truth wherever we go. This should be the longing of our hearts. But if we ever feel discouraged, we need to remember Jesus. He preached and taught only the truth of God and He ended up on a cross. He loved and served and He was still rejected. Even His closest followers abandoned Him and denied Him at His greatest moment of need.

I sometimes wonder if Jesus looked out over the crowd as He hung on the cross and wondered, "Did the seed really take? Was it wasted?" But on that cross Jesus decided to take His nail-pierced hand and toss one more seed. Because maybe, just maybe, the hardened criminal dying next to him had a heart made of soil that was ready. And just maybe the seed would take root, as only God's seed can, and blossom into eternal life right then and there. And it did! Jesus, with some of the last breath He had in His body, let this man know that He would spend forever in paradise. Never lose hope. Let your life and heart be soft as God's seed grows in you and then spread the seed freely and generously.

Session Two—Overcoming Resentment

MATTHEW 20:1–16

Questions 1–3

In Jesus' day it was common practice for those who needed work to wait in the marketplace with their tools and hope that someone would hire them for the day. In this way, these day laborers would make enough money to provide for their loved ones for another day.

This entire parable is based on a contractual relationship between a landowner who hired people for a day's work and a day's wage. This was certainly the case for the first group of workers that were hired. The landowner promised a pay of one denarius for a day of work. In those days, a common workday lasted twelve hours. The laborers would have been expected to perform hard physical labor under the heat of the sun for a full day.

If you follow the parable closely, you realize that the first group hired began their labor at six o'clock in the morning and put in a full twelve-hour day. The second group hired began their work at nine o'clock in the morning and put in a nine-hour day. The next wave of workers did not come on until about lunchtime and worked only six hours. The second to the last group may not have really broken a sweat. They did not begin their labor in the field until three in the afternoon, after the long hot hours of the day. They worked for only three hours, but they did fulfil their commitment to finish out the balance of the work day.

We need to note that, from the beginning, the landowner established two different payment plans. The first group that went out into the labor fields at six o'clock in the morning, as the sun was first rising, were on a clear contract program. They were on a wage plan and would be paid a full denarius for the day of work. It was commonly understood that a denarius was a fair wage for a fair and full day of labor. When these laborers were hired out of the marketplace first thing in the morning, they would have felt they were being fairly compensated for their efforts.

The next three waves of workers were hired under a whole different program. The landowner came to them and asked them to work the balance of the day and promised to pay them "whatever is right" (Matthew 20:4). Now, how much is that? How much are they promised? We don't know.

Near the end of the day, the eleventh hour of this grueling twelve-hour workday, at five o'clock in the evening, just before the quitting-time whistle blew, the landowner went out to see if there were still more people in the marketplace who were not working. After a quick conversation with them, he sent yet one more group out to his fields to work.

This group of laborers were unskilled workers who were living one step above the poverty line every day. Here they were, near the end of the day, hoping someone would come along and hire them. They had their tools, just in case. These laborers were in no position to bargain about wage. The clock was ticking, and their time seemed to be up!

Questions 4–5

This parable is answering the question, "Who is eligible for entry into the kingdom of heaven?" Who can be a child of God? Who is invited to live in the Father's house?

The answer is . . . anyone.

All kinds of outcasts began coming to Jesus—prostitutes, tax collectors, Gentiles, and every kind of sinful person you can imagine. First, it was a small trickle and later a flood. There were those in Jesus' day who were not happy with this arrangement. Some of the religious establishment had a real problem with this upside down approach to kingdom economics. They resented the fact that they had worked so hard, denied themselves the choice fruits of sin, and performed their religious duties with such devotion and now Jesus was inviting sinners to come and sit at the same banquet table. Here came a bunch of latecomers—ragamuffins, sinners, and bedraggled refugees—who were bellying right up to the kingdom banquet table with dirty hands and Jesus was just smiling and letting them in!

Questions 8–9

Some people were envious because Jesus was generous with sinners, but this was nothing new. In the Old Testament we are told that Saul "eyed David" at a certain point because David had become so popular. He was jealous of him. Resentment was also the driving force behind Cain's murder of his brother Abel; he was jealous that his brother's sacrifice was better than his own. Matthew tells us that the chief priests wanted Jesus dead because they were envious of Him.

Those who had worked from the first hour of the morning, who had put in the full day, did not really want the latecomers to get a full day of pay. They would have been happy if the latecomers got nothing, or at least significantly less than they were going to receive. We need to guard our hearts and be sure the poison of resentment does not begin to flow through our veins.

Question 10

This story is not really about the lucky latecomers; the central character in this story is about the master of the vineyard. This landowner keeps going back to the marketplace over and over and over again, even at the eleventh hour. He knows He will receive hardly any benefit for His investment. The other vineyard owners will laugh at him, "Keep that up and you will go broke! It will cost you everything you have."

And they would be right.

But the master of the vineyard can't stop hoping that maybe he would find one more laborer, someone with no prospects, no hope, someone who thinks he will never be selected as a worker. The master of the vineyard hopes that maybe he will fine someone who will be just desperate or hopeful or brave enough to trust him. And if he does, the master will give him a place in his vineyard. Little does the worker know that when payday comes around, the master will give him the full measure of his grace. The loving, generous landowner thinks, "I can't wait to see the look on his face when that happens."

The clock is running out, and any reasonable vineyard owner would have gone home and said enough. But not this vineyard owner, not our God. He keeps coming, looking and hoping for just one more person. Seeking. Searching. Looking for even one last latecomer upon whom He can lavish His grace.

The question is, who will help Him search?

The answer is, you and me. Will we be a church of the open vineyard or a hothouse of performance-based Christianity? God longs for us to be people overwhelmed and undone and humbled by His amazing grace. He invites us to keep noticing grace and keep basking in His love and serving in His vineyard. Now it is our turn to keep going back to the marketplace hoping for just one more worker (see Matthew 9:35–38). And if we find one, we are to invite that person to come work at our side until the day when the Master of the vineyard calls us together and gives us all more than we could ever deserve or dream.

Session Three—Don't Wait Until It's Too Late

MATTHEW 25:1–13

Question 1

This is a story of what might be the two saddest words in the English language: Too Late.

In the parable we will study in this session Jesus is calling us to be prepared. The time will come when we walk in and it will be the final day. There will be no more time to study. The door will be shut. That's it. Either we are ready or it's too late.

In this story there is a group of virgins who have one task: to be ready for the groom when he came.

Question 2

To understand this story we need to understand that back in the first century weddings in Israel could go on for days. There were all kinds of festivities and, at the end, the groom would come to the home of the bride to escort her to the final ceremony. After the formal recognition of their union, the dance would begin.

In our day the full attention of the guests at a wedding is on the bride. The high point of a wedding is when the bride walks down the aisle. In Jesus' day it was just the opposite. All attention was focused on the groom as he came to receive his bride. The way this worked was that before the groom would arrive, a figure called "the friend of the groom" would precede him. He would go to the home of the bride or wherever the wedding party was gathered and say, "Look, here comes the bridegroom. Come up to meet him!"

Because of the importance placed on the bridegroom in Jesus' time, it is pivotal to the story that we find out that the bridegroom is delayed (v. 5). We don't know how long, but it is not forever, and he is coming back. The bridegroom in the story is representative of Jesus, the Messiah, and His return for us, His bride.

This is not just a story for those who will be alive when Jesus returns, it is also for those who will live in the intervening years from His ascension to heaven and His return. The point is that one day the bridegroom is coming back. On that day justice will roll down like water, all of the wrongs on this world will be set right, and we will know the truth about the whole world. Everything will be brought to light. History is not some random cycle of events leading nowhere, nor are our lives just some random searches for pleasure and comfort. We have a story we are writing, and it will have an end and we will be judged. We need to live in the light of this great truth.

The lamp and the oil that the bride is told to keep ready can be seen as our own preparation for Jesus' return. We are being called to the one thing that matters most in all of life: being ready to meet Jesus. We need to be ready when the festivities begin and the bridegroom arrives. Jesus put it this way, "Seek first the kingdom of God and his righteousness." We need to make sure we have lived in such a way that when our life is viewed from God's perspective, we can be confident that it was lived wisely and well.

The story continues. The bridegroom arrives. It is midnight. But five of the brides are not prepared. They have no oil. The other five have their oil ready. When this happens, the five who are not prepared look to the five who have oil and ask if they can borrow some of theirs. But the five who are ready to meet the groom say no. This might seem selfish and unkind, but this is not the point at all. As put by the great Bible commentator William Barclay, "There are some things that can not be borrowed!" A relationship with God cannot be borrowed, character cannot be borrowed, a life cannot be borrowed.

Question 3

It will be helpful to note here that the core message of this passage is about being ready for the return of Jesus Christ. The call to preparedness is first and foremost about being ready to meet Jesus face to face. At the same time, the theme of being ready and living without regret in many areas of our lives is also central in Scripture. For the remainder of this session we will turn our attention to the parallel theme of learning to live without regret in some very practical areas. The goal will be to help us identify ways we can live so that when we do meet Jesus face to face we will not have regrets but joy in how we have invested our one and only life.

One day we will all stand before the living God with our one and only life and we will not be able to lean over to someone else and say, "You know, this decade of my life was pretty empty. Can I borrow a few years from you?" It just doesn't work that way.

Jesus is driving home with brutal honesty the truth we all try to evade: We are each responsible before God for our own life. There are certain factors people can't control, like their genes, but there is a spark within each person called the will that dictates the ability to choose good or evil, love or hate, selfishness or generosity. Each person makes hundreds of choices a day that are knitting the fabric of our soul, and we can't borrow these from anyone else.

There is a deeper truth. It is possible to wait until it is too late. One day the door is going to shut on our lives. The bridesmaids discovered this reality. The groom was late. It looked like they had all the time in the world. Now the moment was at hand and they were not prepared. They had no oil, nor could they borrow oil from anyone else. So they sought to buy some. But it was midnight and the market was closed. They were simply too late. The banquet was beginning, the door was closing, and they were on the outside. The unprepared virgins stand as an example to all of us that time is unspeakably precious and relentlessly short.

How do people end up failing to be ready for the one thing their life really needs to be about? Note that the five who did not have their oil (the unprepared ones) are not called wicked or evil, they are called foolish (v. 8). If you were to ask them, "Why didn't you bring oil for your lamp? Why weren't you ready for the one thing in life that really matters?" they would probably say what kids say when they get caught off guard—"I don't know." These five virgins were not defiant. They are not shaking their fists in the face of God. They don't even make a decision to not follow God. They just never got around to it. This is profound insight from Jesus about how our lives can just slip through our fingers.

We need to heed this warning, the warning of this parable, so that we too don't one day utter the words, "Too late . . . if only." How terrible to reach the end of life and ask, "Why did I spend my one and only life running too fast, or collapsed in front of a television, or obsessing over security, pleasure or power? Why didn't I devote myself to knowing God more fully and intimately? Why didn't I lavish love on my children? Why didn't I pray great prayers? Why didn't I nurture my gifts and use them freely to help build the kingdom? Why didn't I take great risks for Christ? Why did I fritter away my one and only life going like a robot from day to day just punching the clock? Why wasn't I prepared for the return of the groom?"

Spiritual complacency . . . it strikes at the heart of human beings, even those in the church. But Jesus says that the day is going to come when we will see that being prepared for the coming of the groom is the only thing that will really matter. And on that day, may none of us have to say, "I don't know what I did with my life."

Questions 4–6

When we begin to talk about finances and people's personal possessions, all kinds of defenses can crop up. Those who have fears that God wants to take away all of their stuff or that the church is after their money begin to get very uncomfortable when this topic arises. However, the Bible raises issues over and over again regarding how we are to invest our resources. God wants us to live with a deep and profound understanding that all we have is a gift from His hand and that we need to be ready to offer it all back to Him. If we do, we will begin to learn the wisdom of Jesus about storing up our treasure in heaven. If we don't, we may end up living with regret about how we have invested the resources God has placed in our care.

Some are crushed by debt and can't even imagine being generous toward God and His work. It might be time to face this head on and begin to deal with this problem. Others have never tried the discipline of tithing. It might be time to give to God what is rightfully His. Some have committed to tithing but have never allowed God to stretch them beyond tithing to giving. It might be time to listen to God on this issue. Still others may have never developed a heart for the poor. They might need to spend some time investing in a ministry that will expose them to those with great needs in our society. Don't let yourself come to the end of life and miss the great joy of generously and cheerfully sharing in the things that will matter for eternity.

Questions 7–9

Cain did not resist his sinful impulses, he acted on them. This was the first in a heartbreaking chain reaction of sins recorded in the Old Testament that destroyed lives, families, and whole communities. Sin is devastating. The Bible tells us that Cain was hidden from the face of God. Due to his sin, he is cut off from community. Cain's response was, "My punishment is more than I can bear" (Genesis 4:13). He flees from the holiness of God and becomes a fugitive and a wanderer.

Some of us need to start praying about how to do everything possible to see that sin is rooted out of our life by the power of God. Maybe some particular sin has been done in secret and it is time to enter into a time of honest confession to God, to yourself, and to a trusted Christian friend. Maybe you need support but you have never put yourself in a group of people where there can be consistent and firm accountability. Humble yourself, tell the truth about your area of struggle, and get yourself into a place of intense accountability.

You will need to commit yourself to daily time in prayer, seeking the face of God, and crying out for the power that He wants to supply through the Holy Spirit. Reflect with brutal honesty on the implications and possible consequences if you continue to engage in this particular area of sin. Take a blank piece of paper and write down the consequence on every part of your life: your spiritual life, your health, your family, your ministry, your reputation, God's reputation, your witness to those outside of the family, and all the other consequences of this sin.

Questions 10–11

How is God calling you to trust Him? What risks does God want you to take? What steps of faith do you need to take?

Maybe God wants you to take a vocational risk. Maybe God is calling you to a deeper level of boldness in witnessing, or maybe He is calling you to a new area of ministry in your local church. Whatever the area, you don't want to get to the end of your life and be filled with regret that you missed an opportunity God had for you. Don't play it so safe that you never step across the border into the Promised Land.

Session Four—An Invitation to Return Home

LUKE 15:11–24

Questions 1–3

All of us choose at one time or another whether or not we will live at home with the Father or will wander in a distant land. In this parable Jesus tells a story of a son who makes a conscious choice to leave his father and try to make it on his own with disastrous results. Along the way, the boy comes to four crossroads. These crossroads represent stages in his life.

Thankfully, his father was radically different than any father who has ever walked the face of this earth. His seeking love and deep forgiveness made it possible for the son to come home and find a place of restoration and new life. As we dig into this parable it is critical to see ourselves in this story. We are the wandering child and the Father is none other than the God who loves us.

Questions 4–6

We each will face this crossroad at one time or another in our spiritual journey. We will be nagged by the feeling that we would be happier if we went our own way. We come to a point where we don't trust that staying home with the Father will provide the best life for us. Some in your small group may be having these thoughts right now.

Some are considering entering a relationship they know will dishonor God. They know it will not bring lasting joy, but right now they think it will bring love or happiness or pleasure, so they want to leave home so they can do things their own way.

Others are tired of being faithful in a task or a ministry or as a parent. They think that if they could only escape and run away they would be happier. Still others are growing tired of honoring God through faithful giving and tithing and being honest in their business dealings. They are thinking that if they take shortcuts they would be better off and have more to enjoy. They are tempted to leave home financially.

But here is the reality. The son in this story (who represents each one of us) never thinks things all the way through. He sees the allure of temptation but doesn't consider the costs or consequences of that temptation. He never envisions himself far from home, cut off from the love of the father, alone and unloved.

When we come to the crossroad of enticement and temptation, we need to think things all the way through. If we are unfaithful in our relational life, if we bail out on a ministry or responsibility, if we sacrifice our financial integrity, do we really think we will get to the end of life without regretting it?

Questions 7–8

In the story, the son goes to his father and asks for his inheritance so that he can leave home right away. It is very important that we understand the nature of this request. It is not the story of a young man who is out to appropriately assert his independence and explore the world. It is one thing to know what you will get when the will is read, it is another thing to ask for it while your parents are still living.

Ken Baily is a missionary and New Testament scholar who lives in the Middle East. He writes some wonderful materials on the parables and here is one of his insights about this story: "For fifteen years I have been asking people of all walks of life from Morocco to India, from Turkey to the Sudan about the implications of a son's request for his inheritance while his father is still living. The answer is almost always the same. When I ask if anyone in a village has ever made such a request, the answer is 'Never!' Could anyone ever make such a request? The answer, 'Impossible!' If anyone ever did, what would happen? 'His father would beat him, of course.' Why? 'The request means that he wants his father to die.'"

In effect, the son is coming to the father and saying, "I want what is coming to me when you die, and I don't want to wait that long to get it. I want to live as if you were dead right now."

For us, to choose to live in the distant country of sin is, in effect, to say to the Father, "I want to live as if you are dead. I want to live as if you have no claim on my life."

In some ways, the most remarkable part of this story is what comes next. Instead of banishing or rebuking his son, the father does what would startle every person who heard this story. The father took what was his by right, what would sustain him in his old age, and freely gives it to his son. To Jesus' listeners the whole story bordered on the unbelievable. The son had made an outrageous request and the father does the unthinkable in response—he allows the son to leave. This is a total offense to a Jewish father. He was shamed by this rebellious son in front of the entire community. For this son to return would require a Jewish father to ignore the custom of banishing his son from the community.

Here is a God who gives freedom to His children. Here is a whole new kind of love. God, our Father, does what will cause Him immense pain because He hungers so deeply to be in a love relationship with free children.

Questions 9–10

Sin loves to move quickly. Once we have considered the temptation and then made the decision to enter in, action follows right away. In just a few days the son was packed and ready to go. He knew he would be rejected by the whole community for what he had done, so he takes all he has received from his father and leaves town. Very quickly he squanders it all in wild living. But then he hits the next stage or crossroad—the crossroad of pain. Eventually the son finds himself alone, desperate, and hopeless (v. 14). The question was how would he deal with pain? What would he do when he hit the wall? He had no more money for parties or distractions. He was so desperate that he took a job tending pigs, a job any Jewish person would find unthinkable. It was this place of pain that woke him up to the truth of his condition and the need to return home to the one place he could find healing.

Some of us have areas of pain where God wants to do work in us. Maybe you are in a painful season of your marriage. Maybe you feel unfulfilled in your life. Maybe you are living with the pain of needing to please other people all the time and you feel hollow inside. Maybe the pain is because you have guilt or sin with which you have never really dealt.

Here are your choices. You can mask your pain by distracting yourself and trying to deny it. You can find little moments of happiness to get you from one day to the next. You can watch too much TV, eat too much, spend too much money. You can focus on achievments, or try to please others, or stay so busy you can't think about it. Or you can decide to stop running. You can reflect on the source of your pain and hear the call to come home again.

Session Five—Heart-Healing Forgiveness

LUKE 7:36–50

Answers to Opening Questions:

C and C.

Questions 2–4

To understand the passage we will study in this session we have to be aware of the cultural context and etiquette of the day. As a visiting rabbi, Jesus would have been the guest of honor. It was considered an act of merit to invite a rabbi to your home. In a setting like this, there were certain rules that could be taken for granted. For instance, the customary greeting for an honored guest would have been a kiss. If the guest was a person of equal social rank, the host would greet the guest with a kiss on the cheek. If the guest was a person of very high rank, the host would kiss his hand. To neglect this would have been like having people come into our home today and not say hello, shake their hands, or even acknowledge them at all.

Another part of first-century Middle East etiquette involved the washing of feet. This was mandatory before meals. Because feet were commonly dirty, it was standard practice to offer a footwashing as guests arrived. If your guest was of a very high status, the host would wash the guest's feet as part of the greeting and as a sign of reverence. If the guest was of an equal social standing, a servant would wash the guest's feet. An optional practice in Jesus' day when an honored guest came over was to offer olive oil to anoint the guest's head.

When we realize that Simon had done none of these things, we begin to fully understand the explosive and tense setting. Everyone at the table would have felt great unease at the breaches in custom that were occurring.

In those days, banquets were often a public affair. They were often set in a courtyard of a well-to-do person. In this setting, anyone could walk up and watch and listen, and many did. While uninvited guests could not sit at the table, they could view and listen from nearby.

It is very likely that the woman in this story had heard Jesus teaching in the village earlier that day and was drawn to this place to hear more. Something about Jesus struck her deeply. It may be that she had begun to reflect on her own life and how she had ended up. No one ever plans to end up as a prostitute. At one time she had been someone's little girl. Once she was the object of her mother's hopes and dreams. But somewhere along the way everything had changed.

Maybe her husband had rejected her and this was the only way she could survive financially. Perhaps her heart had grown hard and cold and she simply did not care anymore. However it happened, she had heard Jesus teach and something inside of her broke. She came to a point of realizing that even she, in the midst of her sinful condition, was loved by God. It was not too late for her.

Now, we can be certain that she would not have been invited to a dinner like this, not at the home of a Pharisee. You can only imagine how much courage it took for her to even enter the courtyard. But when she gets there she sees Jesus and is undone by love. She watches as Jesus is shunned by Simon. She sees that He is not greeted with a kiss, His feet are not washed, and that no one anoints Him. She knows that she can't be the one to give Him a kiss of greeting—it would be presumptuous. Then the thought comes, maybe as an impulse, that she could kiss His feet. To wash His feet would be an act of humility. To kiss them was abasing.

Try to picture the scene. Jesus is reclining at the table. In those days the table would be real low, close to the ground, and people sat not on chairs but on cushions. They reclined at the table and propped themselves up with an elbow. Their heads were near the table and their feet were extended away from the table.

The woman comes and stands at His feet. You can be certain everyone was watching her, particularly Simon. She kneels down to kiss His feet. She looks at Jesus and instead of judgment and ridicule or embarrassment, she sees indescribable love. She has not seen that look in a man's eyes for a long time, maybe ever. Here is someone who loves her not in the shadows but in the light; not in hiding but in the open. She is so overwhelmed that tears begin to flow. Before she can do anything, they are just pouring down her face. Tears of sadness for what she has done in her past and tears of gratitude because Jesus offers forgiveness. Tears of unbelievable joy because a whole new life lays ahead for her.

In those days women always kept their hair up. To let their hair down in public was considered too sexually provocative. This was taken so seriously that if a married woman let her hair down in front of a man other than her husband, it was grounds for divorce. As we realize this custom, and the reality that the people at the table most likely knew what this woman did for a living, what happened next is shocking. She let her hair down right there in front of everyone. In her lifetime she had let her hair down far too many times and with too many men. But now she lets her hair down for the last time and uses it to dry her own tears off Jesus' feet.

Luke tells us that she had an alabaster jar of ointment. Most likely this refers to a flask that was often worn around the neck as a kind of perfume for women. Again, because of her profession this flask was quite important. She had certainly used it a drop at a time with many men, but now she empties the whole thing! She will not need it anymore. She knows that anointing Jesus' head would be presumptuous because He is a holy man and she is a sinful woman. But she pours it over His feet—all she has, her whole life. She just pours herself out with no shame in extravagant adoration and gratitude.

Questions 5–7

Simon is watching his banquet not turning out at all as he had planned. He says to himself, "I guess Jesus must not be anything special because if He was a prophet, He would never let a woman of her reputation touch Him with a ten-foot pole." But Jesus knew all about who the woman was and he also knew all about Simon.

So Jesus tells Simon that He has something to say to him. The sense of the language is that Simon will not like hearing what Jesus is about to say. Simon had not only wrongly judged this woman and Jesus, there is also a sense that he is exalting himself in his own heart and mind. So Jesus tells him a parable to help put all that is happening into perspective.

Questions 8–10

This woman has boldly loved Jesus. She has gone out on the limb of her life and has poured out her tears, her kisses, her ointment, her very heart. Can you imagine her eyes as Jesus turned and looked at her? I imagine their eyes locking: the Savior and the sinner. The Rabbi and the prostitute. Her eyes must have been filled with a whole lifetime of emotion: embarrassment, shame, a sense of unworthiness, but mostly just radiant love. And Jesus' eyes were filled with love and grace. Jesus, her champion and advocate, looked right at her and spoke words that must have poured over her with healing power.

Can you imagine the feeling that came upon this woman when Jesus said, "I tell you, her sins which are many are forgiven!" This is newness of life. This is forgiveness. This is healing. This is being born again.

Jesus announces to all the people gathered for the banquet that this woman, this sinner, this one who has so wasted her life, has received grace. That is why she has poured out everything. That is why her tears are flowing, why her hair is down, why her kisses won't stop, and why she has poured out the very last drop of her perfume. She has come to know that she is forgiven much and that is why she loves so much.

Jesus closes His lesson by turning Simon's eyes back to himself. Jesus is sensitive enough to refrain from telling Simon that he is the one who loves little, but then again, that would only be stating the obvious. Jesus lets him know that those who believe they have little to be forgiven will only love a little bit. And Simon has to figure out that the shoe fits on him.

The problem is that Simon perceives himself as one who needs very little forgiveness. In his heart of hearts, he feels God is getting a pretty good deal with him. Simon does not love much because he sees himself as a person with few debts toward God. When he looks at the sinful woman at Jesus' feet, he sees her as the one with a big debt. He is filled with spiritual pride and superiority.

The greatest commandment is to love God and love our neighbor. By contrast, the greatest sin is to refuse to demonstrate love and therefore to disobey the greatest commandment. Jesus is saying, "Simon, don't you see? You are the biggest debtor of all!" If only Simon could see it and fall to the ground in a humble heap beside this woman and see himself as just as needy as she is, he could be changed forever. If only his tears would flow and his hands serve. Then he could see that this sinful woman is a sister in the fellowship of forgiven debtors.

At the end of the day, this parable is not about the differences between Simon and the woman. Jesus is speaking these words to help Simon see that the two of them are the same. The woman needed grace for a heart that was broken and Simon needed grace for a heart that was hard. Who is the big debtor? It was her! It was him! It is me! It is you! We are the debtors, and it is time we realize that and feel it to the core of our being.

Session Six—Spiritual Sincerity

MATTHEW 21:28–32

Questions 2–3

In Jesus' day family life and work life were intimately connected. It was a matter of economical survival that sons were expected to work for their father. So it's no surprise when, at the start of the day, the father gives instructions to his sons for the day's work.

In this parable we see two sons. One is rebellious but ends up coming to work for the day. A second son is compliant, willing, and enthusiastic but has no intention of doing the father's will. By the end of the day we discover that the second son never entered in the vineyard and the role for which he was created. He never put his hand to the work for which he was made.

After telling the story Jesus asks the crowd which one of these sons truly did the will of the father. His point in making this application is to show that His story of going to the vineyard was a metaphorical way to talk about doing the will of God and being conformed to the image of Christ.

Question 4

It is very important for group members to seriously consider identifying an area in which they feel called to grow deeper in spiritual sincerity. We all have areas in our lives in which we are not conformed to the heart and will of Christ. It can be our tongue, our temper, or a poor attitude. We all have areas in which we are not following the will of Christ . . . in which we are not getting to the vineyard.

The first stage in the process of character formation involves the ministry of confrontation. We need to gain a sense of clarity of where we are not conformed to the image of Christ. Maybe you see a pattern of deceit in your life. Maybe it is the way you relate to your spouse. Maybe you are dealing with greed in your finances. Maybe you are damaging people through your words or actions. Perhaps you have habits that are out of control. We all have areas where we are not working in the vineyard and not following the will of the Father.

Questions 5–6

How does the ministry of confrontation come to us? Sometimes it comes through Scripture. God speaks with power through the Word, and it can show you an area in which there needs to be change. Almost every follower of Christ can recall a time when this has happened. As we read the Scriptures we need to actually ask God to do this work of confrontation by His Holy Spirit. Then we need to respond and repent.

Sometimes a breakthrough occurs in corporate worship. God's people are gathered, the Holy Spirit is present and moving, and your heart is tender so that the Holy Spirit begins to work, to speak, to do spiritual surgery as only He can do. It might be through a line in a worship song, during a time of corporate prayer, or in a moment of silence. The question is, will you listen when God speaks in these moments?

Sometimes a breakthrough comes through the teaching of God's Word. A pastor, Bible study, or small group teacher opens the Word and God begins to speak to you. You hear a biblical challenge and you feel an elbow right in the ribs. You know this message is for you. This "ministry of the elbow" can come from someone sitting next to you or it can come from the Holy Spirit. It makes you realize that God is saying this word is for you and it is time to repent and change. Every time you gather with God's people, ask God to speak by His Spirit.

Sometimes it even comes through an unbeliever. I remember a time years ago when I was driving in my car. I have to admit that I was not driving a way in which Jesus would have been pleased. As I raced along someone pulled up next to me, rolled down his window and shouted, "What's your problem?" Then he drove off. It might sound strange, but the question has stuck with me for years, every time I get in my car. He did not stick around to help me sort out my problem, but God used him to raise the question. Sometimes God speaks through a person you don't know and who may not even know God. Be open and ready to receive what God wants to say through these people.

God also chooses to speak through a brother or sister who knows and loves you. God often calls us to change through a person with whom we are closely connected and who is willing to share truth with us. I remember a two-day period when I spent a concentrated amount of time with a small group of four friends. During these days I made a point of asking each one of these people, "What is an area in my life I need to be working on and where I am not in conformity to the image of Christ?" Every one of them spoke openly with me. There was one area of my life that all four mentioned. As they spoke, I knew they were right. These were like John the Baptist to me, close enough to know me and speak the truth. We all need people like this in our lives.

When someone has this ministry in your life, you will usually recognize it. When they point out an area in which you need to grow, you will often say to yourself, "Yes, that makes sense to me." What you realize is that you have been aware of this area where you need to grow, but you have been living with it for so long you have become numb to that part of your character.

Questions 7–8

In the parable we are studying, we can be like the first son. We can harden our heart, close our eyes, and deliberately shut out God. Many followers of Christ do exactly this. But we need to remember how his day ended. The first son's heart softened. His attitude changed. His love for the father and the father's love for him won out and he turned around and went to live in the vineyard. He repented and followed the father's will. This is the only way to live.

The only response that will bring health and wholeness in our lives is to say yes to the Father and then live it out. God will not force us into His will. If we resist and defy Him, we will have our way. But He gives us every opportunity to open our heart and say yes to Him.

Let God know you are willing and ready to do whatever needs to happen to bring your life into conformity with His will. Even if it means someone else needs to know the truth about you, stop resisting, debating, and denying. Ask for God to do His work in you and change you. Acknowledge your need for the Holy Spirit to fill you anew and grant strength for a changed life. Turn around and head for the vineyard.

Questions 9–10

This kind of change does not happen overnight. We can't microwave transformation into the image of Christ; it is a process that takes time. Usually, as God is working in us we are called to enter the practice of certain spiritual disciplines through which God brings about change. Here are some examples:

- If a person has a spirit of joylessness, their discipline might be daily, joy-filled singing.
- If a person's heart is cold toward God, maybe the discipline needs to be talking with the Father, praying and adoring Him every day.

- A person who talks too much may need to develop a discipline of silence.
- A person who deals with fear needs to take an appropriate risk and step out in faith.

Whatever the area, there are practical changes and daily disciplines that will help you grow in spiritual sincerity.

Willow Creek Association

Vision, Training, Resources for Prevailing Churches

This resource was created to serve you and to help you in building a local church that prevails!

Since 1992, the Willow Creek Association (WCA) has been linking like-minded, action-oriented churches with each other and with strategic vision, training, and resources. Now a worldwide network of over 6,400 churches from more than ninety denominations, the WCA works to equip Member Churches and others with the tools needed to build prevailing churches. Our desire is to inspire, equip, and encourage Christian leaders to build biblically functioning churches that reach increasing numbers of unchurched people, not just with innovations from Willow Creek Community Church in South Barrington, Illinois, but from any church in the world that has experienced God-given breakthroughs.

Willow Creek Conferences

Each year, thousands of local church leaders, staff and volunteers—from WCA Member Churches and others—attend one of our conferences or training events. Conferences offered on the Willow Creek campus in South Barrington, Illinois, include:

Prevailing Church Conference: Foundational training for staff and volunteers working to build a prevailing local church.

Prevailing Church Workshops: More than fifty strategic, day-long workshops covering seven topic areas that represent key characteristics of a prevailing church; offered twice each year.

Promiseland Conference: Children's ministries; infant through fifth grade.

Student Ministries Conference: Junior and senior high ministries.

Willow Creek Arts Conference: Vision and training for Christian artists using their gifts in the ministries of local churches.

Leadership Summit: Envisioning and equipping Christians with leadership gifts and responsibilities; broadcast live via satellite to eighteen cities across North America.

Contagious Evangelism Conference: Encouragement and training for churches and church leaders who want to be strategic in reaching lost people for Christ.

Small Groups Conference: Exploring how developing a church *of* small groups can play a vital role in developing authentic Christian community that leads to spiritual transformation.

To find out more about WCA conferences, visit our website at www.willowcreek.com.

Prevailing Church Regional Workshops

Each year the WCA team leads several, two-day training events in select cities across the United States. Some twenty day-long workshops are offered in topic areas including leadership, next-generation ministries, small groups, arts and worship, evangelism, spiritual gifts, financial stewardship, and spiritual formation. These events make quality training more accessible and affordable to larger groups of staff and volunteers.

To find out more about Prevailing Church Regional Workshops, visit our website at www.willowcreek.com.

Willow Creek Resources™

Churches can look to Willow Creek Resources™ for a trusted channel of ministry tools in areas of leadership, evangelism, spiritual gifts, small groups, drama, contemporary music, financial stewardship, spiritual transformation, and more. For ordering information, call (800) 570-9812 or visit our website at www.willowcreek.com.

WCA Membership

Membership in the Willow Creek Association as well as attendance at WCA Conferences is for churches, ministries, and leaders who hold to a historic, orthodox understanding of biblical Christianity. The annual church membership fee of $249 provides substantial discounts for your entire team on all conferences and Willow Creek Resources, networking opportunities with other outreach-oriented churches, a bimonthly newsletter, a subscription to the *Defining Moments* monthly audio journal for leaders, and more.

To find out more about WCA membership, visit our website at www.willowcreek.com.

WillowNet (www.willowcreek.com)

This Internet resource service provides access to hundreds of Willow Creek messages, drama scripts, songs, videos, and multimedia ideas. The system allows you to sort through these elements and download them for a fee.

Our website also provides detailed information on the Willow Creek Association, Willow Creek Community Church, WCA membership, conferences, training events, resources, and more.

WillowCharts.com (www.willowcharts.com)

Designed for local church worship leaders and musicians, WillowCharts.com provides online access to hundreds of music charts and chart components, including choir, orchestral, and horn sections, as well as rehearsal tracks and video streaming of Willow Creek Community Church performances.

The NET (http://studentministry.willowcreek.com)

The NET is an online training and resource center designed by and for student ministry leaders. It provides an inside look at the structure, vision, and mission of prevailing student ministries from around the world. The NET gives leaders access to complete programming elements, including message outlines, dramas, small group questions, and more. An indispensable resource and networking tool for prevailing student ministry leaders!

Contact the Willow Creek Association

If you have comments or questions, or would like to find out more about WCA events or resources, please contact us:

Willow Creek Association
P.O. Box 3188, Barrington, IL 60011-3188
Phone: (800) 570-9812 or (847) 765-0070
Fax (888) 922-0035 or (847) 765-5046
Web: www.willowcreek.com

Continue building your new community!

New Community Series

Bill Hybels and John Ortberg

with Kevin and Sherry Harney

If you enjoyed this New Community Bible Study Guide, look for these others!.

Exodus: ***Journey Toward God***	0-310-22771-2
Parables: ***Imagine Life God's Way***	0-310-22881-6
Sermon on the Mount[1]: ***Connect with God***	0-310-22884-0
Sermon on the Mount[2]: ***Connect with Others***	0-310-22883-2
Acts: ***Build Community***	0-310-22770-4
Romans: ***Find Freedom***	0-310-22765-8
Philippians: ***Run the Race***	0-310-22766-6
Colossians: ***Discover the New You***	0-310-22769-0
James: ***Live Wisely***	0-310-22767-4
1 Peter: ***Stand Strong***	0-310-22773-9
1 John: ***Love Each Other***	0-310-22768-2
Revelation: ***Experience God's Power***	0-310-22882-4

Look for New Community at your local Christian bookstore or by calling 800-727-3480.

www.willowcreek.org

GRAND RAPIDS, MICHIGAN 49530

www.zondervan.com